FUTURE
FORWARD FAITH

7 Days of Believing God
Right Now *for* ***What's Next***

RAINAH DAVIS

Book Project Management by Raindrop Creative, Inc. | StartWrite Publish Team

Editorial Team: Tiara Brown | Tara Crews | Amira Allen-Alston | Dr. Erin Almond

Cover Art: Raindrop Creative Design Team: Donovan Purvey/Rainah Davis

978-1-970179-95-8 Paperback
978-1-970179-94-1 eBook

This book is a part of the Activate Your Faith Devotional Series.

Activate Your Faith: The Art of Facing Fiery Trials

978-1-970179-77-4 Paperback
978-1-970179-04-0 eBook

The other two books in the series are:

Faith Foundation: 7 Days of Facing Fears and Overcoming Doubts

978-1-970179-90-3 Paperback
978-1-970179-91-0 eBook

Fragments: 7 Days of Fixing Fractured Faith

978-1-970179-90-3 Paperback
978-1-970179-91-0 eBook

DEDICATION

To my parents – Gerald & Ruby Simmons. God knew, before the beginning of my life, the exact DNA I would need to be who He created me to be on the Earth. While none of us are perfect, I am eternally grateful that, out of all the parents I could have been given, He chose to give me to you.

I have emerged from seasons that others could not have survived. While that is a testimony of my perseverance, it is also evidence of what you instilled in me. My faith is strong, the foundation of my existence, and that is in large part due to how you and my grandparents have raised me.

The words "thank you" seem inadequate, but appropriate. I love you, and I pray that all I do for our family, our community, and the world makes you as proud of me as I am to call you "Dad and Mom." Every battle you fought and won has empowered me to encourage others to have "future-forward faith."

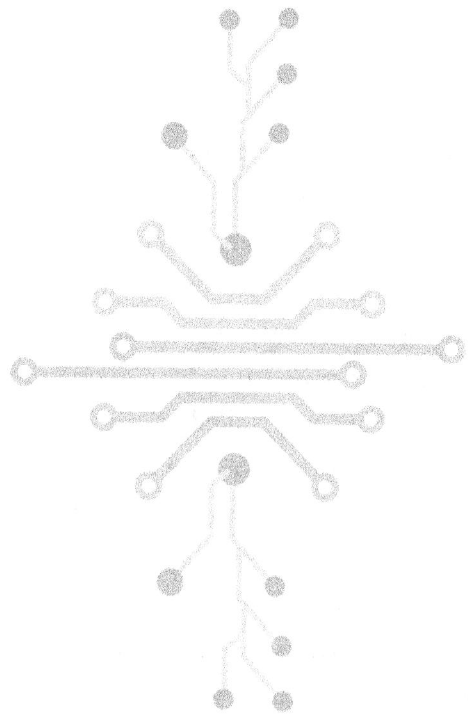

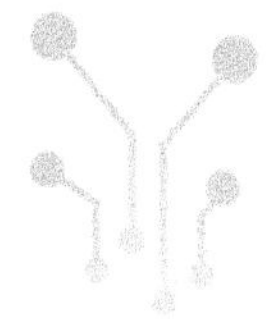

TABLE OF CONTENTS

PREFACE

Special note: *If you have read either devotional (Faith Foundations or Fragments), you can skip this section and begin at "Day 1 – Following Faith." The following material (Author's Note, Introduction, When God Says No, Two Keys to Overcoming Temptation, and Devotion III Overview: Future Forward Faith) is included for those new to the Activate Your Faith series.*

This devotional has been rewritten three times. The version in your hands was the one God knew you would need at this time. The original chapters have been sliced and redistributed to teach you the art of facing every trial in the Activate Your Faith book series. The book is divided into three segments to clarify the different aspects of faith. Each week, you will have a daily devotion that ties to a theme for that timeframe:

Week 1 – Section 1: Faith Foundation: *7 Days of Facing Fears and Eliminating Doubts*

Week 2 – Section 2: Fragments of Faith: *7 Days of Fixing Fractured Faith*

Week 3 – Section 3: Future Forward Faith: 7 Days of Believing God **Right Now** *for* **What's Next**

The devotional in your hands is the third segment (7 days) of a 21-day devotional. I was compelled to make each section its own seven-day devotional, so you would not have to wait until the entire book is available.

Now, more than likely, you are grown. Therefore, I am not telling you what to do, and I would not dare try! All of my children are adults, so I know grown people will do what they want (smile). However, I recommend you block off the next 7 days and go through this devotional in a quiet place. Also, I encourage you to do the activities at the end of each day.

I would love for you to do a personal mini-Bible study on the Biblical encounters and historical references that stand out to you. Studying the art of anything is to approach it from a multi-faceted level. Also, the art of facing trials with fiery faith strategically and psychologically prepares you to minimize damage and resource waste. This knowledge is vital because before you can win a battle, you must survive it. Since we will face struggles in this life, the idea is to meet each challenge with boldness and strength, relying on your faith in God. This book will serve as a powerful tool in your arsenal against the fiery trials attempting to quench your faith.

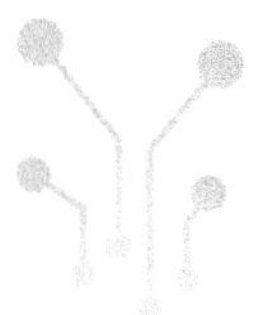

AUTHOR'S NOTE

As I write the third intro to this book, I am in awe of God's providence and timing. Six years ago this month, I was released from my job. As the days passed and months rolled in and out, it would be years before I understood why God would have allowed that event to occur.

Maybe you, like me, are staring at the face of a fiery trial in real-time. If so, then I have good news for you. There is an art to facing fiery trials. The way a pianist's fingers glide over the ivory keys, or a relay runner completes a good baton handoff during track and field events, is the same type of rhythm and execution needed to activate your faith.

I am in the midst of another transition as I pen these words to you. God has burdened me to complete this book in this specific season. Many of the personal stories you will read in this work are years old, but the principles I learned and will share with you are sound. It is an honor to join you, arm in arm, through the fire.

I assure you that the Lord is with us, and when we come out, there will not be a hint of smoke on us. I love you, and I am cheering for you. So, let's get started!

—Rainah

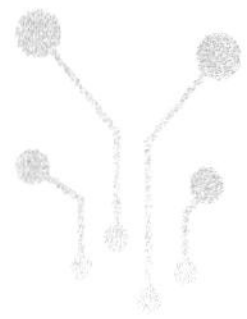

INTRODUCTION

I started this devotional series almost ten years ago and have added to it every few years. Clearly other projects have taken priority over it, until now! In November 2019, I was blessed to see Todd Galberth, my good friend, brother, and the author of the foreword to Activate Your Faith, create a dynamic worship experience for his live recording. Listening to him share his powerful testimony and the faith it took to produce this anointed and majestic experience inspired me to complete this unfinished work.

I had just released another Activate book designed to educate and empower individuals to develop the mindset necessary to start their businesses. During Todd's recording, I realized that no matter what industry a person is in, it takes faith to step out and do something extraordinary with passion and guts! I was in awe as I remembered God had allowed us to remain connected for almost a decade. I met Todd at World Overcomers Christian Church, where we both worked. He was one of the church's dynamic worship leaders. I vividly recall worshiping and crying out to God during his worship sets. In truth, his energetic, anointed, and intense praise and worship services helped me make it through one of the worst storms of my life. Therefore, it seemed fitting to include him in this book. Shortly after, I started working on the book but was halted again by the COVID-19 pandemic that shut down the entire world.

In the fall of 2022, Todd released a single from the album I mentioned above called "He Won't Fail." The song ministered to me profoundly, and I was prompted once again to complete this book. A few days later, I told my business coach about it, and she challenged me to finish it in seven days. And so I did. Now, I am finally set to complete the series. I want to thank you for being a part of the journey and I pray that this book will bless you. Now, let's get into it!

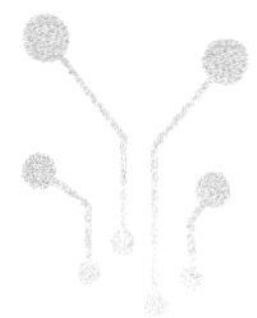

WHEN GOD SAYS NO

In 2010, I faced the most difficult trial of my life—the burial of a marriage that had figuratively died, decayed, and rotted many years earlier. I spent years praying, fasting, and begging God to revive and resurrect a relationship that was no longer beneficial for me. Thankfully, God denied my requests and pleas in an evident and final way. Although devastated, I yielded to the undeniable "No" I had heard from the Heavens. I began preparing my daughters and me for an unexpected move for them, unaware of it.

In December 2010, I stepped out on faith and moved into a tiny house with my four daughters, ages fourteen to five. However, praise be unto God; at first, we survived, and then we **thrived**. Today, at the time of this writing, not only am I remarried, but I am also the absolute happiest I have ever been.

For years, I battled against the depression that convinced me I would lose my mind. Seriously, the enemy had me convinced that I would eventually end up having what my grandmother used to refer to as "a mental breakdown," which would leave me locked up in a padded cell and wearing a straitjacket for the rest of my life. However, as the hit gospel duo so eloquently put it: "But He didn't see fit to let none of these things be… You keep on, keeping on, keeping me…" (Artist: Mary Mary/Song: "Thank You"/2002 Incredible Album). God kept me and brought me out stronger than ever.

Now I have a testimony! The same way God kept me, He can keep you, as the old saints would say, "He'll keep you when you can't keep yourself!" God is a "keeper," and I have experienced His "keeping power," which is so astounding that I want to help you experience it, too.

During the next 7 days, my goal is to help you face whatever trials you are experiencing with fearless faith and abundant joy. The Book of James admonishes us in James 1, verses 2-4: "My brethren, count it all joy when you fall into various trials, knowing that the testing of your faith produces patience. But let patience have its perfect work, that you may be perfect and complete, lacking nothing."

Then in 1 Peter 4, verses 12-13 we read: "Beloved, do not think it strange concerning the fiery trial which is to try you, as though some strange thing happened to you; but rejoice to the extent that you partake of Christ's sufferings, that when His glory is revealed, you may also be glad with exceeding joy."

The passage in James reveals that "the trial" truly has a purpose and that if we yield to the purpose of "this trial," we actually gain "perfection and completion." In 1 Peter, we are instructed not to be caught off guard when trials approach us because our partaking in suffering, as our Savior did, will result in our having "exceeding joy" once His glory is revealed. Hence, the Bible is clear that we should embrace trials. We should face fiery trials, knowing there is a purpose at the end of the tribulation.

Unfortunately, this directive is much easier said than followed. So, over the next 7 days, I want to help you develop the skill set to face your trials with fearless faith, knowing that God will bring you out of every difficulty you face. There is an art to facing trials, specifically the fiery ones that we believe were sent to take us out!

Before I give you a formula for enduring the test, I must inform you that there are different kinds of trials. The Word admonishes us that in all our getting, we need to endeavor to get an understanding. Understanding is often the difference between enduring something and breaking under the pressure it produces.

There are three basic kinds of trials that you will face during your Christian walk:

1. TRIAL TYPE #1 – Discipline from the Lord, based on previous sin or natural consequences based on unwise decisions.

2. TRIAL TYPE #2 – Persecution and suffering for living a Christian life.

3. TRIAL TYPE #3 – Attacks and temptation from demonic forces sent to distract or destroy you.

Trial Type #1

The first trial type is the easiest for a mature believer to accept. Every mature saint can recount decisions that have landed them in a devastating situation. Mature people of God who face financial difficulty because of mismanagement of money conclude that "satan didn't steal their rent money." Mature believers can admit that they spent it on "miscellaneous" items, which are frivolous or unplanned expenses that can be hard to pinpoint at the end of the budget cycle. This type of trial is a direct result of the individual's behavior, and it carries consequences. *For example:*

» If you don't pay your rent or mortgage = you will no longer have a place to stay.

» If you cheat on your spouse repeatedly = you will eventually lose your spouse.

» If you miss too many days of work = you will lose your job at some point.

» If you get too many speeding tickets and don't drive at safe speeds = you could ultimately lose your license, your car, or your life.

There are also spiritual consequences for sin. The Word warns us that the wages of sin are death. We must be diligent in making better spiritual decisions, so we don't jeopardize our relationship with Christ.

Many believers repeatedly find themselves in a cycle of chastening from the Lord or reaping the consequences of destructive life "choices." It is vitally important that we master sin and make good decisions, because this is the only trial we have control over in our lives. The other two are based on God's permission or permissive will. Trial type is reduced or even eliminated based on your decisions. I encourage you to break the cycle of consequences you find yourself in by asking the Lord to help you with your decision-making. We will discuss this matter in more detail throughout this book.

Trial Type #2

The second type of trial we face is inevitable. John 15:18-20, NIV reveals: "If the world hates you, keep in mind that it hated Me first. If you belonged to the world, it would love you as its own. As it is, you do not belong to the world, but I have chosen you out of the world. That is why the world hates you. Remember what I told you: 'A servant is not greater than his master.' If they persecuted Me, they will persecute you also..."

This Scripture informs us that every believer will suffer because of their faith. It isn't popular preaching; therefore, many speakers and ministers do not adequately remind us of this spiritual "fallout," but it is still the truth. A relationship with Christ doesn't give you a "trouble-free life" pass. In fact, the more havoc you wreak on the kingdom of satan, you may find that the attacks against you often increase. When this counterattack occurs, you must get closer to the Lord and ensure that you don't allow the trial to push you further away. In truth, once you reach maturity and are unshakeable in your Christian walk, the enemy will often attack you or those closest to you. "The weakest links" in your life will take hits designed to impact or stop you. These types of attacks usually accompany the last kind of trial.

Trial Type #3

The third type of trial we face is the kind that makes us the most upset and is the most often assumed. When we first receive salvation, we believe that every challenge comes from our adversary, satan. However, as we mature in Christ, we learn that not everything is of the devil. Yet, because we know that even Jesus was tempted by satan, the enemy is coming for us. The Word defines satan's assignment quite explicitly as "kill, steal, and destroy."

This assignment doesn't need any further definition and leaves little to the imagination. The old saints taught us that the Bible says, "*When* your day of evil comes," and not "*If* your day of evil comes," because each of us has a day of evil that will surely come.

The Bible is also explicit on how to handle this type of trial. There are so many verses that minister to us on overcoming temptation. We will explore some of them more in-depth throughout our 21-day journey together.

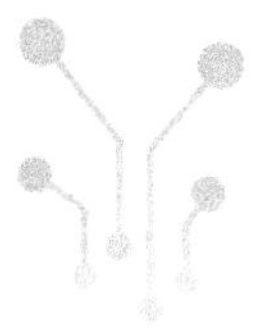

TWO KEYS TO OVERCOMING TEMPTATION

In the following Scriptures, there are some main points I want you to meditate upon:

"No temptation has overtaken you that is not common to man. God is faithful, and He will not let you be tempted beyond your ability, but with the temptation, He will also provide a way of escape, that you may be able to endure it."
—1 Corinthians 10:13, ESV

"Submit yourselves, therefore, to God. Resist the devil, and he will flee from you."
—James 4:7, ESV

I

God will provide a way of escape from the temptation you face. I am amazed at how often God offers us ways of escape that we choose to ignore. I am also throwing myself under the bus. If we are honest, we have all fallen short of the glory on this one! When He sends an interruption (like a phone call or a knock at the door) right before you are about to give someone a "piece of your mind," you should let yourself be interrupted. Please don't ignore the call or the knocking: yield to it. Often, some of the worst experiences we have faced involve interruptions when we were about to fall into temptation. Still, we ignored the interference that was sent to save us. When we submit ourselves to God and resist temptation, that temptation has no choice but to flee from us.

"Finally, be strong in the Lord and in the strength of His might. Put on the whole armor of God, that you may be able to stand against the schemes of the devil. For we do not wrestle against flesh and blood, but against the rulers, against the authorities, against the cosmic powers over this present darkness, against the spiritual forces of evil in the heavenly places. Therefore, take up the whole armor of God, that you may be able to withstand in the evil day, and having done all, to stand firm."
—Ephesians 6:10-13, ESV

II

God has given us armor, so we should put it on! Decide to be strong in the Lord because you are fighting against the armies of hell. God has given us all access to armor we can put on to withstand enemy attacks. This armor helps protect you so you can stand firm, fight bravely, and win against all evil forces.

Now that you have a basic description of the types of trials we face and what God expects of us as we meet them head-on. Let's learn how to face these trials with fearless faith, then use our knowledge to help others do the same. We will do this by learning about the different types of faith that our Biblical ancestors applied to the challenges they faced. Every kind of faith provides the art form of facing and overcoming fiery trials.

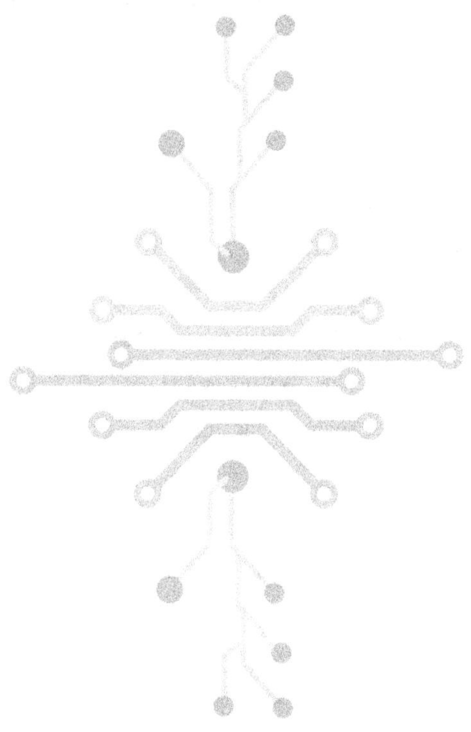

DEVOTIONAL III
OVERVIEW

When Everything Shakes but God Stands

Listen, family – I need you to hear me clearly. As I'm writing this, we have just come through one of the most challenging seasons in recent history. And when I say challenging, I mean it with my whole chest.

We've watched systems shake in real time. We've seen government shutdowns that froze paychecks and left more than a million federal workers in limbo. Some were furloughed. Others were working without pay, trying to decide between gas, groceries, or keeping the lights on.

On top of that, tens of millions of people who rely on the Supplemental Nutrition Assistance Program (SNAP) – our current-day food stamp system – held their breath, wondering if the benefits that fed their families would suddenly vanish. Parents were looking at pantries and babies at the same time, doing math that did not add up. Food banks were stretched, then stretched again.

Meanwhile, flights were delayed or cancelled because air traffic controllers and TSA agents were calling out – some literally couldn't afford gas to get to work. Medical appointments were missed. Important trips were postponed. The whole nation felt the tension and the tightness.

And even if that specific shutdown didn't hit your house, you've felt your own shaking:

+ A pandemic that rearranged life as you knew it.
+ A layoff that came out of nowhere.

- A diagnosis that shook your body *and* your faith.
- A personal crisis that never made the news – but almost broke you.

Whether it's a shutdown, a pandemic, a layoff, or a private storm that only you and God know about – you now know what it feels like when **systems fail, but God doesn't**.

Because here's the testimony, I'm standing on with everything within me: through every day of that chaos, every sleepless night, every unpaid bill, every cancelled plan – **HE. KEPT. US.**

Divine Timing for Your Next Season

Now, I don't think it's an accident that it has taken me nearly two years to finish this devotional. I wholeheartedly believe God **held** this part until this precise moment. This isn't a coincidence – this is **His divine timing**.

Right now, as we're catching our breath from what we've just lived through, the question is not: *"Will there ever be another storm?"* We already know the answer to that. Life will *life*.

The real question is: *"How will we respond when it comes?"* Will we spend the next few years bracing ourselves in fear, scrolling in anxiety, waiting for the next crisis to hit?

Or will we **activate our faith for our NEXT right now** – and partner with God to prepare, build, and position ourselves for whatever comes? This devotional is your invitation to choose the second option.

From "Late" to "On Time:"
A Story About Divine Timing

Let me show you exactly what I mean. Last December, my youngest daughter looked at me and asked, "Mom, are we going to church for New Year's Eve? Are we going to Watch Night?"

Now, a little background: we live between two states. When we're in Georgia, we attend Change Church – Dr. Dharius Daniels is our pastor. For that particular holiday, it was looking like we'd be in Georgia. So, my daughter pressed me, the way children raised in church do when they catch you slipping: "Mom, we're going to be here. We *should* go."

I need to confess something to you: I am a bit of a **digital disciple**. After working in church for decades and traveling as much as I do, I have gotten really comfortable watching online in my leggings with my blanket and my beverage.

But that gentle nudge from my baby? I could not shake it. So, I said, "Okay. *Let's go.*" We left with fifteen to twenty minutes to spare – enough time (in theory) to park and walk in comfortably. But about fifteen minutes away from the building, we hit a WALL of traffic. We couldn't even turn into the parking lot. By the time we finally parked, the service had already been going for twenty-five minutes.

At that point, we had options:

1. Turn around and drive the hour back home, grumbling.
2. Or stay put and see what God might be up to.

Something in my spirit said, **"Stay."** So, we parked. We walked to a nearby pizza place. (It was brisk outside, but not unbearable.) We ate. We laughed. We people-watched. We waited. We didn't want to lose our parking spot, and honestly, we weren't sure what else to do.

Turns out, we ended up being thirty-five minutes early for the **next** service – the one, I am now convinced, we were **destined** to be at.

When we walked in, the theme on the screen read: **AN-CHOR.** That word stopped me in my tracks. I had ministered on "anchor" before. There's Scripture; there's a song. And to see it as the theme for the night felt like a direct wink from heaven.

But what happened next took me all the way out. When Dr. Dharius stepped up to the podium, the first thing he said was: **"This is the year you FINISH."**

I nearly slid out of my seat. One minute I was rejoicing, the next I was fighting tears. Because the book you're holding in your hands? **It was on my list of things to finish.** And I felt late. I felt behind. I felt like I missed my window – that everyone else finished their thing on time, and I was somewhere back at the starting line with a pen, a laptop, and a pile of half-done ideas.

But right there in that service, I made a list of everything I was going to finish in 2025. And now, as we come to the end of that year, **I have finished this book.** Here's the testimony: not only do you need to be in the right place at the right time, you also need to be willing to **listen to who God uses to get**

you there. God used my daughter to push me into that specific service at that specific time. Anyone who watches multiple services knows everything doesn't happen the same way twice. Had I watched online later, I might never have heard that word in that way.

> **You are not late.**
> **You are not behind.**
> **You are right. On. Time.**

There's a God Part, and There's a You Part

Here's the revelation that ties this all together – and it came through one of my mentors. They told me to think about what happened that night:

There was a **God part**:

+ He allowed the traffic.
+ He held the word "*anchor*" for that service.
+ He put "*This is the year you finish,*" in my pastor's mouth at the exact moment I needed to hear it.

And there was a **me part**:

+ I had to listen to my daughter's nudge.
+ I had to get dressed and go.
+ I had to choose to stay when turning around would've been easier.

✦ I had to sit in that sanctuary with a tender heart and an open notebook.

We shout over the fact that God loves us. We celebrate that He is faithful. We quote Hebrews 13:5 – that He will never leave us nor forsake us. And all of that is true. But beloved, that's not the whole testimony.

> **Yes, God kept you.**
> **Yes, God covered you.**
> **Yes, God is carrying you.**

But He is also **inviting you to partner with Him.**

God will do the supernatural – but He will often use your **natural decisions** as the vehicle to carry those blessings. That means:

✦ **There's a *God part* in sustaining your finances.** And there's a *you part* in setting a budget, saving when you can, and obeying when He nudges you to start that side business.

✦ **There's a *God part* in protecting your family.** And there's a *you part* in setting boundaries, getting wills and insurance in order, and having those "we don't want to talk about it, but we need to talk about it" conversations.

✦ **There's a *God part* in your mental health and emotional stability.** And there's a *you part* in going to therapy, honoring your capacity, and saying "no" when your calendar (and your nervous system) are already at capacity.

> **Prayer is not a substitute for preparation.**
> **Prayer is the power source for preparation.**

Future Forward Faith says, "I'm not just asking God to show up – I'm also going to show up for the life He's calling me to."

From "Just Surviving" to Strategic Faith

In the toughest seasons of life, many of us are just trying to make it through the week – sometimes, just through the day. And listen: that's valid. When the ground under you is shifting, survival is a real, holy thing.

But once the immediate storm passes, we cannot just exhale, wipe our brows, and slide back into the same patterns that had us unprepared in the first place. We are not only called to **survive** – we are called to **steward**.

We're living in a moment as significant as the printing press, the Industrial Revolution, and the early internet. We cannot afford to sleepwalk through this era. We must be people who ask:

+ *"Lord, what does wisdom look like in this season?"*
+ *"What do I need to build now so my family is safer later?"*
+ *"How can my faith shape the way I budget, save, study, rest, and show up?"*

That's **Future Forward Faith**.

It's not fear-based hoarding – it's faith-based planning.

It's not panic – it's preparation with God's perspective.

Your "All Gas, No Brakes" Moment

Here's my challenge to you: **Pick ONE thing to go all in on.** Just **one**. Not twenty. Not your whole life in a week. Not "I'm going to fix my money, my marriage, my diet, my prayer life, my business, my closet, and my group chat by Friday." **One**. One area where you're giving God **all gas, no brakes**.

And because I love you, let me clarify: When I say "all gas," I do *not* mean grind until you collapse. I mean **wholehearted, obedient effort** in the lane God has actually called you to, trusting Him to be the brakes if you start to veer off track.

Maybe your "one thing" is finally starting that business you've been dreaming about.

Maybe it's finishing the degree you put on pause. Perhaps it's getting into therapy and staying long enough to see a real breakthrough – and if that's you, hear me: **there is NO shame in that game. Your mental health IS health.**

Maybe your one thing is your body – choosing to move more, sleep more, and nourish yourself well. For me? I picked **health and wellness.**

In March 2025, I began my weight-loss and wellness journey with a focused approach. Not because I wanted to squeeze back into some random dress from 2012, but because I want to live well – for my husband, my children, my grandchildren, my parents, and the women I'm called to pour into.

Let me keep it all the way real: this journey has not been a straight line. There was a point when I had lost 24 pounds, then gained a little, but I got right back on track and saw I was down another 25.5 pounds (yes, we count every ounce)! But seriously, here's the truth: when I first saw those numbers going in the wrong direction, I wanted to throw the whole scale into the sea of forgetfulness, never to be remembered again.

Yet, here's what I realized: that wobble – that back and forth – that "up-down-what-is-this-scale-doing-today?" That's not failure. That's the **process**.

The win is that I stayed in the game. I kept walking. Kept lifting. Kept hydrating. Kept choosing better foods. Kept working on my sleep. And something powerful happened: The discipline I was building with my body became a skill I could use in every area of my life.

Your body is not just a temple – it's your assignment vehicle. Your health is part of your wealth, family. Invest in it now so you can show up fully for the future God is calling you into.

The Prayer for This Season

Let me give you a prayer for this season of your life – a prayer that rises from a place of courage, not fear: *"Lord, I don't have the wisdom or the knowledge to see everything that's coming. But You do. So here's my commitment: I'm going to give You all gas, and*

I'm trusting You to be the brakes. Stop me if I'm out of alignment. Slow me down if I'm moving in the wrong direction. Accelerate me when I'm in step with Your will. If it's not You, I don't want it. And if it is You, I can't be stopped."

This is not the time to shrink back just because life has been hard. This is the time to step into **faith-fueled strategy**. This is where your **trust in God** meets your **daily decisions**. This is where **survival** turns into **stewardship** – where human limitation meets divine possibility.

The Time Is NOW

Sometimes, God allows "shakings" to reveal what's truly stable. Every storm you've been through, every season you barely crawled out of, every stretch that made you wonder if you had anything left – it all showed you what can be shaken, and what cannot.

Your **job** can be shaken.

Your **schedule** can be shaken.

Your **plans** can be shaken.

But your **God cannot be shaken**.

The very fact that you are reading this right now means you made it through something that could have taken you out. What looked like a delay was actually divine timing. God wanted you to read this after you had lived through some shaking – so you wouldn't just nod and say "Amen," but so you would recognize your own story on these pages.

Wherever you are, I'm here as your sister, your coach, and your faith friend to speak this over your next season: What the enemy meant for evil, God is turning for good.

What **shook** you is not going to **sink** you. What **delayed** you does not **disqualify** you. Every storm, every setback, every "no," every detour – God is weaving all of it into your testimony and your triumph.

Pick your **one** thing. **Commit to it**. And watch God multiply your discipline into destiny.

Your Future Forward Faith Journey

So, buckle up, family. Over the next seven days, we're moving from just hoping for the future to partnering with God for it. You're going to walk with:

- A young widow who followed her bitter, grieving mother-in-law into an unknown land.
- A woman who poured out her soul in a temple until her tears became the watering ground for a prophet.
- A dreamer who went from pit to prison to palace and learned how to store up in plenty for the famine ahead.
- And three young men who stood in a fire hotter than anything you've faced – and came out without even the smell of smoke.

I won't spoil all the details now. Just know this: each day will give you a different facet of **Future Forward Faith** – how you follow, how you pray, how you plan, and how you stand when the heat is on.

You don't have to know everything that's coming next. You just need to walk with the God who does – and be willing to act on what He shows you. Let's build this Future Forward Faith **together**.

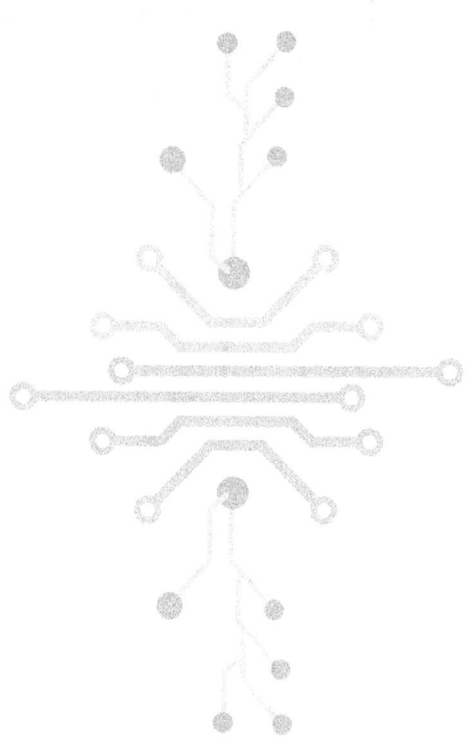

DAY 1

FOLLOWING FAITH

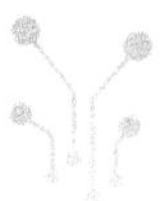

The Strategic Power of
Covenant Following

Following /ˈfɑːloʊɪŋ/ – *verb*
To move forward in the same direction as someone who has gone before; to accept someone's leadership with intentional commitment and strategic purpose.

Kingdom Definition: A Spirit-led posture of covenant alignment where you intentionally follow God in others and the path He sets, so your steps are positioned for His favor, formation, and generational impact.

Following Faith Scripture Foundation:
Ruth 1:16–17 (NLT)

¹⁶ But Ruth replied, "Don't ask me to leave you and turn back. Wherever you go, I will go; wherever you live, I will live. Your people will be my people, and your God will be my God. ¹⁷ Wherever you die, I will die, and there I will be buried. May the Lord punish me severely if I allow anything but death to separate us!'

> **Big Idea:** Your future won't just be shaped by what you lead – it will be radically shaped by **who** and **how** you choose to follow.

We live in a culture that worships the Superwoman myth and the self-made story. Do it all. Hold it all. Lead it all. Be the strong one, the smart one, the one everybody calls when life falls apart. On top of that, the world tells you, "If you didn't do it by yourself, it doesn't count." Here's the truth: **no one who has built anything great did it alone.**

I once heard Daymond John say, "Every overnight success typically took a minimum of fifteen years."Fifteen years of help. Fifteen years of guidance. Fifteen years of mentors, teachers, elders, critics, coaches, and community. Fifteen years of following someone – often in hidden seasons, inconvenient seasons, and "this doesn't make sense yet" seasons.

The real question isn't, *"Am I following?"* We all are. The real question is: **Who am I following – and is this alignment**

pushing me toward God's future for my life or pulling me away from it?

We say, "A leader without followers is just somebody taking a walk." That's true.

But here's the other side: **A follower without discernment? That's somebody walking straight into a ditch.**

Future-forward faith invites you to lay down the "I got it all by myself" cape and ask: "Lord, who have You called me to follow in this season – and at what level?"

When God Moves in an Unexpected Way

In grad school, I took a class called *Leadership Communication,* and that's where I first heard the word "*followership.*" Not just leadership – **followership.** I was shocked it even existed. Then I learned there were actual types and levels of followers.

Around that same time, I heard a preacher teach about the man at the pool of Bethesda. At the end of his message, he asked a question that hit me right in the chest: "Do you want your miracle badly enough to receive it in a way you didn't expect?" Sit with that for a second. What if God wants to bless you:

+ In a way you couldn't script.
+ Through a person you wouldn't have chosen.
+ In a place you never planned to be.

Sometimes, the miracle is on the other side of following God down a path that makes absolutely no sense to your natural mind. Sometimes, it comes through following an unlikely leader – a mentor, a spouse, a child, a boss, a pastor – who doesn't fit your picture of "who should be in charge."

I've watched that play out in my own life. There have been moments when someone in my family – like my oldest daughter – had to take the lead on a situation, and the rest of us had to follow her wisdom. That is humbling when you're used to being the one in charge.

But that's the beauty and tension of following faith: sometimes, the person you're called to follow looks younger, less experienced, or even a little unsure. Yet God is using them to guide you.

Ruth's Revolutionary Following

Ruth is a brilliant case study in this. In Ruth chapter 1, we meet Naomi, her husband Elimelech, and their two sons. There is a famine in Bethlehem – ironically called the "House of Bread." Instead of staying put and trusting God to provide in the famine, they moved to Moab. On the surface, it looks logical: "No food here, food over there. Let's go."

But hear this: **not every open door is a God door.** Sometimes, instead of standing firm in a hard season, we run. We switch jobs, switch churches, switch cities, switch relationships – and step out of the very place God intended to bless us *after* the storm passed. The famine didn't last forever. By the time Naomi returns later, Bethlehem has bread again.

But in Moab, tragedy hits:

+ Naomi's husband dies.
+ Then both of her sons die.

Naomi is left with her two Moabite daughters-in-law: Orpah and Ruth.

When she hears there's provision again in Bethlehem, Naomi decides to go back home. The daughters-in-law start the journey with her, but at some point, Naomi stops and says, "Girls, listen. I love you, but let's be real. I'm too old to give you more sons. Even if I did, you wouldn't wait for them to grow up. Go home. Go back to your people. Remarry. Start over. I'm praying God will be kind to you."

On the surface, it sounds noble and selfless. But grief is complicated. Sometimes, people push you away not only to protect you, but because they're exhausted and want to be alone with their pain.

Orpah resists for a moment – she cries, she clings – but as soon as Naomi releases her again, she kisses her goodbye and goes back.

That's the "Are you sure, Mommy? I don't mind doing the dishes…okay, bye!" child. She offered. You declined. She's gone. That's Orpah.

Ruth, on the other hand, feels a holy tug that says, **"Stay."** Her response is so powerful, we still use it in wedding ceremonies around the world: *"Don't ask me to leave you and turn back. Wherever you go, I will go; wherever you live, I will live. Your people will be my people, and your God will be my God.*

Wherever you die, I will die, and there I will be buried…" (Ruth 1:16–17). This is not casual. This is a covenant **language.** This is a diehard **following.** Ruth chooses to follow Naomi:

+ Away from her comfort zone.
+ Away from her familiar culture.
+ Away from the possibility of a "fresh start" with one of her own people.

And into a future she cannot see – with a grieving woman who doesn't look like a "success story."

But Ruth isn't just following Naomi, the woman. She is following the **God** she met through Naomi's family. That's **Future Forward Faith.**

The Levels of Following Faith

In that grad school class, I learned that not all following is the same. There are levels and types. Spiritually, we see this play out in how we respond to God and the people He places in our lives. These follower styles can help you locate yourself:

1. **Isolates** – Present but disconnected. In the building but not in the Body – too guarded to risk disappointment, so they don't truly follow anyone.

2. **Bystanders** – Watching but not moving. They see God moving for others but won't step in for themselves. This is Orpah energy: thankful for the journey, but gone when it gets uncomfortable.

3. **Participants** – Helpful but hesitant. They'll support the vision when it's convenient, but you won't find them in the hard, hidden, messy places that require sacrifice.

4. **Activists** – Engaged and invested. This is that Ruth energy – motivated by purpose, showing up even when the leader is in a valley season, even when the strategy doesn't make sense yet.

5. **Diehards** – Covenant followers. "Where you die, I will die." They're committed not just to the person but to the assignment of God in that person's life, even when the path is unclear.

Future-forward faith doesn't just ask, "Who am I leading?" It also asks, "Who has God called me to follow – and how deeply?"

Following the God in Them (Even When They Look a Mess)

If we're honest, Naomi would not have made your Top Five "follow this woman" list. She's grieving. She's bitter enough to rename herself "Mara" (bitter). She's convinced God has dealt harshly with her. She is not posting inspirational quotes and "soft life" pics on Instagram. She looks like a walking testimony of, "How did we get here?"

But Ruth sees something deeper. Yes, Naomi is broken. Yes, Naomi is exhausted. Yes, some of Naomi's decisions (like leaving Bethlehem during a famine) may have contributed to where they are now. And yet, Naomi still carries a covenant. She still carries **history with God.** She still carries **wisdom** that will guide Ruth into her next chapter.

Sometimes, God uses people who are in the middle of their own meltdown to lead you into your miracle. That's why that preacher's question matters so much: "Do you want your miracle badly enough to receive it in a way you didn't expect?"

What if the person God is using to help shift your future is:

+ Older, slower, and not "plugged in" like you?
+ Younger, less seasoned, and not as polished as you'd like?
+ Still working through their own trauma, grief, or healing?

Ruth chose to follow **God shown in Naomi**, not the brokenness of Naomi.

There are places where you met God – jobs, churches, relationships, programs – that weren't perfect. Some of the people there might have been the reason you almost left. But that doesn't erase the fact that **God found you there.** Sometimes, you are exactly where you're supposed to be, even if the people who got you there are not perfectly representing the God you met in that place.

The Strategy in Your Submission

There is a difference between blind following and strategic positioning. Ruth wasn't following everybody. She made a calculated,

Spirit-led decision to follow **one** woman into an unknown land. Look at the pattern of her following:

+ **She followed Naomi from famine to feast.** Ruth leaves Moab and returns to Bethlehem – the House of Bread – right as the famine lifts. Timing matters.

+ **She followed Naomi's wisdom about work.** Ruth doesn't sit at home scrolling and sulking. She basically says, *"Somebody has to work."* She goes to glean in the fields, doing hard, humble labor to provide for them. In a world chasing shortcuts and soft life with nothing built yet, Ruth is like, *"Let me grab this barley!"*

+ **She followed Naomi's insight about relationships.** When Naomi realizes Ruth has "happened" into the field of a relative named Boaz and keeps coming home with extra grain, the matchmaking auntie in her wakes up. Naomi gives very specific instructions about how Ruth should position herself. Ruth doesn't roll her eyes and say, *"Ma'am, you haven't dated in forever."* She follows the instructions.

+ **She followed without constant commentary or pushback.** In a world where everyone has an opinion, a clapback, and a comment, Ruth chose a quieter strength. She listened, she considered, and she submitted to Naomi's wisdom without needing to argue, adjust, or add her own spin at every turn. At any point, Ruth could have said, "You got us into this mess. I'm not listening to you." Instead, she honors Naomi's position and experience, even while Naomi processes her pain.

On the other side of that faithful following, Ruth ends up:
+ Protected and provided for in Boaz's field,
+ Covered by a man who honors her integrity,
+ And ultimately in the **bloodline of Jesus Christ.**

And all of that started with one decision: "I'm going to follow this woman where she's going and follow her God as my God."

Your covenant decisions – who you follow, who you align with, whose wisdom you submit to – have long-term and legacy implications. Your followership is literally writing part of your family's future.

The Modern-Day Application

Let's bring this concept into your life right now. Some of you said yes to a job, church, or relationship, thinking you were following a great leader – and now you see major flaws, and you're wrestling with disappointment.

God is nudging some of you to submit to a process, a mentor, or a season that doesn't look glamorous and doesn't give you instant results. Following can feel heavy when leadership isn't perfect. It's hard to follow a spouse after they've broken your trust. It's hard to follow a supervisor who's inconsistent.

It's hard to follow a pastor who is human and visibly struggling through their own valley.

Here are your anchors:

+ You are **not** called to follow everyone.
+ You are **not** called to follow foolishness.
+ You *are* called to follow Jesus – and sometimes, He leads you through imperfect people into perfect alignment.

This is where discernment and boundaries matter. Future-forward faith doesn't make you a doormat. It makes you **discerning and strategic.** Ask yourself:

+ Is this person leading me closer to God or further away?
+ Do they have a real covenant with God, even if they're in a rough season?
+ Am I following their charisma, or the God assignment on their life?

My pastor once preached that God is faithful to us because it's His nature – but He shows an extra layer of faithfulness toward those who are faithful to Him. That stuck with me. When you are a faithful employee, God has a way of sending you faithful employees later. When you are faithful in the assignment He's given you, God has a way of opening doors you could never pry open for yourself.

Over the next few days, we're going to build a different kind of faith – not just faith to survive today, but faith to partner with God for what's next.

Kingdom Strategies for Following Faith

1. Identify Your Field of Favor

Ruth "just so happens" to end up in Boaz's field. In the natural, it looks random. Spiritually, it is divine alignment. You, too, have a **field of favor**:

+ A space, assignment, or community where God has assigned a particular grace to your life.
+ A place where your obedience, work, and presence yield more than they logically should.

Where is God calling you to glean in this season? Is it a local church, a small group, a business, a classroom, a nonprofit, a mastermind, or a healing community? What field keeps coming up in conversation, prayer, or "random" opportunities? Stop trying to work in every field. Ask God to reveal your field of favor and commit to show up there consistently – even when it's not glamorous, even when the work feels small, even when you don't "feel like it."

2. Recognize Your Naomi Voices

Who helps you see God's presence in your life? Not just who makes you feel good. Not who agrees with everything you decide. Who are the *Naomi* voices – the people who:

+ Tell you the truth in love,
+ Remind you who God is when you're tempted to forget,

+ Carry wisdom from their own walk that can shorten your learning curve?

They might be older. They might be younger. They might be going through their own hard season. But something in your spirit knows, "I'm supposed to be connected here."

Don't dismiss people just because they're in a valley. Naomi came home bitter, but she finished her life blessed, with a grandbaby in her arms because of Ruth's faithfulness. Some of the people who look the least "followable" right now may end up being living proof of God's restoration later.

3. Practice Covenant Following

Don't be an Orpah – here today, gone tomorrow. When God confirms who you're supposed to follow in this season, follow with your whole heart. That does **not** mean:

+ You ignore red flags.
+ You abandon boundaries.
+ You tolerate abuse or manipulation.

It **does** mean:

+ You stop "half-following" while secretly keeping one foot out the door.
+ You lean in fully to the process God is using to mature you.
+ You stay until God releases you – not just until your feelings get uncomfortable.

Covenant following sounds like: "Lord, I trust Your leading through this person, and I'm willing to stay the course until You say the season has shifted."

Following Faith Takeaways

1. **Your following determines your field.** Who and what you follow shapes where you end up. Ruth followed Naomi back to Bethlehem and stepped into a field of favor that shifted her entire bloodline.

2. **Favor is found on the other side of faithfulness.** Ruth's consistent, humble following opened the door to provision, protection, and purpose that she could never have manufactured on her own. God is faithful – but He reveals an extra dimension of faithfulness to the faithful.

3. **Strategic submission leads to supernatural elevation.** Ruth's choice to submit to Naomi's wisdom positioned her for a level of elevation she never could have reached by trying to be "self-made" in Moab.

Following Faith Prayer

Lord,

Forgive me for the times I've been an Isolate or a Bystander in Your Kingdom. Give me discernment to recognize the Naomi voices You've placed in my life and grant me the humility to follow when my flesh insists on leading. Show me my field of favor and give me the courage to glean there, even when it's unfamiliar or uncomfortable. I declare that I will not be an Orpah who turns back at the first opportunity. I choose to be a Ruth — steady, faithful, and aligned with Your plan for my future. Position me for covenant connections that will shift my bloodline and align me with the future You've prepared.

In Jesus' name, Amen.

Following Faith Challenge
(with Built-In Journaling)

This week, I want you to do three things:

1. **Name Your Follower Style** – Are you an Isolate, Bystander, Participant, Activist, or Diehard in this season?

   Journal: Where do I see this style showing up – in my church life, family, work, or friendships? How has it helped or hindered my growth?

2. **Identify at Least One Naomi Voice** – Ask God to highlight a person (or two) He's assigned to help guide you in this season – a pastor, mentor, elder, therapist, coach, or friend who pulls you closer to Him.

   Journal: Who has been speaking wisdom into my life that I haven't fully leaned into yet? What fears, pride, or disappointments make it hard for me to receive from them?

3. **Make One Concrete Move of Obedience** – Do something that reflects covenant-level following: join the group, show up to the call, send the email, sow into the vision, sign up for the class, or commit to that process you've been avoiding.

   Journal: What step did I take, and how did it feel to choose faithful following instead of staying safely on the sidelines? Where do I sense God smiling over this step?

> **Remember:** Ruth's "following faith" put her in the genealogy of Jesus. Your obedient following today is setting up blessings for generations you will never meet.

Tomorrow's Teaser:
Faithful Faith with Hannah

Tomorrow, we're sitting with Hannah – a woman whose future-forward faith turned her private pain into a public breakthrough. Get ready to see how persistent, faithful prayer doesn't just change your life; it births a purpose that impacts generations and advances the Kingdom.

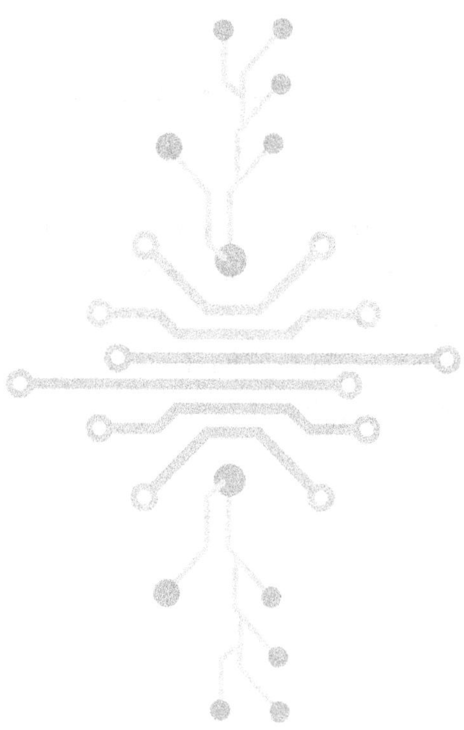

FERTILE FAITH

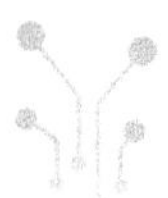

Hannah –
From Barren to Breakthrough

Fertile (FUR-til) – *adjective*
Capable of producing abundant fruit; able to conceive and bring forth; transforming barrenness into a birthplace through persistent, specific, surrendered prayer.

Kingdom Definition: A surrendered heart that allows God to use painful, dry, waiting seasons – watered by specific prayer and obedience – as soil where He births prophetic purpose, generational chainbreakers, and every kind of holy assignment (children, callings, companies, and courage).

Fertile Faith Scripture Foundation:
1 Samuel 1:6–20, ESV

⁶*And her rival used to provoke her grievously to irritate her, because the Lord had closed her womb.* ⁷ *So it went on year by year. As often as she went up to the house of the Lord, she used to provoke her. Therefore Hannah wept and would not eat.* ⁸ *And Elkanah, her husband, said to her, "Hannah, why do you weep? And why do you not eat? And why is your heart sad? Am I not more to you than ten sons?"* ⁹ *After they had eaten and drunk in Shiloh, Hannah rose. Now Eli the priest was sitting on the seat beside the doorpost of the temple of the Lord.* ¹⁰ *She was deeply distressed and prayed to the Lord and wept bitterly.* ¹¹ *And she vowed a vow and said, "O Lord of hosts, if you will indeed look on the affliction of your servant and remember me and not forget your servant, but will give to your servant a son, then I will give him to the Lord all the days of his life, and no razor shall touch his head."* ¹² *As she continued praying before the Lord, Eli observed her mouth.* ¹³ *Hannah was speaking in her heart; only her lips moved, and her voice was not heard. Therefore, Eli took her to be a drunken woman.* ¹⁴ *And Eli said to her, "How long will you go on being drunk? Put your wine away from you."* ¹⁵ *But Hannah answered, "No, my lord, I am a woman troubled in spirit. I have drunk neither wine nor strong drink, but I have been pouring out my soul before the Lord.* ¹⁶ *Do not regard your servant as a worthless woman, for all along I have been speaking out of my great anxiety and vexation."* ¹⁷ *Then Eli answered, "Go in peace, and the God of Israel grant your petition that you have made to him."* ¹⁸ *And she said, "Let your servant*

find favor in your eyes." Then the woman went her way and ate, and her face was no longer sad. [19] *They rose early in the morning and worshiped before the Lord; then they went back to their house at Ramah. And Elkanah knew Hannah his wife, and the Lord remembered her.* [20] *And in due time Hannah conceived and bore a son, and she called his name Samuel, for she said, "I have asked for him from the Lord.*

1 Samuel 2:1-10, ESV

[1] *And Hannah prayed and said, "My heart exults in the Lord; my horn is exalted in the Lord. My mouth derides my enemies, because I rejoice in your salvation.* [2] *"There is none holy like the Lord: for there is none besides you; there is no rock like our God.* [3] *Talk no more so very proudly, let not arrogance come from your mouth; for the Lord is a God of knowledge, and by him actions are weighed.* [4] *The bows of the mighty are broken, but the feeble bind on strength.* [5] *Those who were full have hired themselves out for bread, but those who were hungry have ceased to hunger. The barren has borne seven, but she who has many children is forlorn.* [6] *The Lord kills and brings to life; he brings down to Sheol and raises up.* [7] *The Lord makes poor and makes rich; he brings low and he exalts.* [8] *He raises up the poor from the dust; he lifts the needy from the ash heap to make them sit with princes and inherit a seat of honor. For the pillars of the earth are the Lord's, and on them he has set the world.* [9] *"He will guard the feet of his faithful ones, but the wicked shall be cut off in darkness, for not by might shall a man*

prevail. [10] *The adversaries of the Lord shall be broken to pieces; against them he will thunder in heaven. The Lord will judge the ends of the earth; he will give strength to his king and exalt the horn of his anointed.*

> **Big Idea:** God doesn't waste your wait. Specific, surrendered prayers in wilderness seasons birth purpose that shifts nations and raises generational chainbreakers – whether that shows up in a crib, a classroom, a company, or a calling.

The Story Deep Dive

Let's talk about Hannah: The woman who was loved but lacking, favored but frustrated, chosen but childless. If you've ever been in a season where you have the gifts, the skills, the anointing – but there is one thing that just will not come together, this day is for you.

If there were a reality show called ***Real Housewives of the Bible***, Hannah would be front and center as the first wife, the beloved. She has Elkanah's heart, but her womb is closed. Enter Peninnah, wife number two, in a culture where men often took more than one wife, mainly to ensure children and heirs. Peninnah has what Hannah doesn't – babies. Many of them. And she's loud about it. If this were a TV show, the producers would lean all the way into that tension: the loved-but-barren first wife and the fertile-but-less-favored second wife under the same roof.

Hannah has love, but no children. Peninnah has children, but not the same love. And Peninnah uses her advantage like a weapon. Scripture says her rival provoked her "year after year" until Hannah was reduced to tears and could not eat. Every feast day became a fresh reminder of what she didn't have.

Now bring that reality into today: Everyone else is getting promoted – but you. Everyone else is posting wedding photos – but you. Everyone else's business is "sold out again!" – and you're just trying not to overdraft the account. Everyone else is announcing babies – and you're navigating infertility, miscarriage, or deep grief. Or maybe you've realized that motherhood for you will look like adoption, fostering, auntie life, or mentoring the next generation instead of carrying a child in your body.

The Peninnahs don't just live in your house anymore; they live on your timeline: That cousin at the cookout: "So when you gon' get married?" That auntie at Thanksgiving: "Still no babies yet?" That coworker: "You're still at that level? I thought you'd be further by now." And for many women, these aren't hypothetical scenarios. Roughly 1 in 5 women with no prior births struggle to get pregnant or carry a pregnancy to term. That's nearly 20% of women who know the sting of longing for motherhood or grieving what never came. If that's part of your story, I am so sorry for the ways church people, family, or culture may have added shame on top of your pain.

Additional grief may include: the loss of a spouse, parent, sibling, or even a child. There are women reading this who are loved – and still feel like something in them died with the person they lost. And the reality is, a part of life as you knew it really does end.

Yet, on the other side of that grief, God can birth a different kind of purpose – like the mother who founded Mothers Against Drunk Driving after losing her child, or others who turned unspeakable loss into advocacy and healing work. Hannah shows us what it looks like to be:

> » Loved – and still lacking.
> » Favored – and still frustrated.
> » In covenant with God – and still waiting.

Hannah shows us what it looks like to turn that ache into fertile faith.

The Fertile Ground Truth

Let me drop some farming wisdom that will change how you see this season. My grandfather farmed for over fifty years. We watched seeds go into the ground and disappear for a while – no action on the surface – before they finally pressed through with a harvest. He knew what it took to produce a quality crop, and so did God.

Science tells us it takes around 17 essential elements in the soil for healthy plant growth. If even one is missing, the harvest can be stunted, delayed, or destroyed. So, a field that looks like "nothing is happening" may actually be in a critical preparation phase – being amended, adjusted, and enriched for future fruitfulness.

Now, here's the part that shifts your perspective: One of the earliest and still most effective soil amendments is manure. Yes, that – *waste*. The stuff that stinks. The stuff we try to get rid of as fast as possible. But in the hands of a skilled farmer, even the mess gets recycled as nourishment. Let's translate that: *Every taunt from Peninnah. Every misunderstanding from Eli. Every delay that made you question your worth. Every betrayal, layoff, heartbreak, or "no."* All of it can become fertilizer in the hands of a God who refuses to waste your pain.

My grandfather used to say, "A good watermelon ain't cheap, and a cheap watermelon ain't good." Quality has a cost. Your blessing is not going to be cheap. It will cost you something: your pride, your comfort, your timelines, your image. Fertile faith is grown in soil that has seen some mess.

> **Petty people? Require fertilizer.**
> **Your pain? Requires fertilizer.**
> **Your past? Requires fertilizer.**

On the other side of the stink, the waiting, and the "nothing is happening" days, you and your harvest will both be stronger. You'll know your worth and the worth of what God grew in you.

Three Lessons from Hannah's Fertile Faith

1. You can have less in the natural and still have a double portion in the spiritual.

Hannah's husband gave her a double portion, even though her womb was closed. She was still the beloved. You may not have: The baby, the promotion, the ring, or the booming business, but you still have **favor**.

You can be: Overlooked in one season and remembered in another. Like Joseph in prison, forgotten until the moment his gift was needed, grieving deeply, and still being the one God chooses to carry a life-changing assignment. Sometimes, the absence of the one thing you long for shouts so loudly you forget what you *do* have. Hannah's story whispers: *You are still loved. You are still seen. You are still chosen* – even while you wait, even if your story unfolds differently than you pictured.

2. Your enemy and your tears are fertilizer, not your finale.

Peninnah provoked Hannah year after year. But what if the rival wasn't the real enemy? What if God allowed Peninnah's taunts to push Hannah into a deeper kind of prayer she wouldn't have prayed otherwise? Without Peninnah's persecution, there might not have been that desperate promise: *"Lord, if You give me a son, I will give him back to You all the days of his life."*

Without that prayer, there might not have been a Samuel. Without Samuel, who would have anointed David? Your enemy isn't your end. They're enriching your soil. And your tears? They are not wasted; they are *rain*. Hannah cried and prayed with such intensity that Eli thought she was drunk. She looked wild to people who didn't know the depth of her pain. Yet those tears were watering seeds. In farming, no rain means no harvest. Tears are often irrigation for breakthroughs.

So, if you need to cry – baby, cry. Let it out. Let it flow. You are not weak. You are watering the ground for what's coming. We see this pattern in modern stories, too: The founder of Mothers Against Drunk Driving channeling grief into advocacy. Tyler Perry went from living in his car to owning one of the largest film studios in the U.S. Sara Blakely faced rejection after rejection before building a billion-dollar company. All **manure**. All **rain**. All **used by God**.

3. Determination, discipline, and desire must drive you – NOT drama, desperation, or defeat.

Picture your inner life like a race car. Somebody is behind the wheel. The question is: who? Emotions are bad drivers. Drama is a reckless driver. Desperation will speed you into places God never sent you. Defeat will pull over and quit on the side of the road. Destiny is the driver you want behind the wheel.

Hannah took a destiny drive. She didn't clap back at Peninnah. She didn't drag her rival online. She didn't let bitterness drive her decisions. She took her anguish to God, turned down her plate, and poured out her soul in persistent, specific prayer. When Eli misunderstands her, she doesn't pop off. In a world where everybody has commentary and clapbacks locked and loaded, she listens, responds with respect, and invites spiritual agreement instead of staying stuck in offense.

Then – this is key – when God answers, she keeps her vow. She brings Samuel back and dedicates him to the Lord's service. No reneging. No *never mind, God.* Her follow-through becomes part of why her womb stays open for more children later – and why her story still births courage in us today.

Determination, discipline, and holy desire for God's will drive her to destiny.

The Modern-Day Application

Fertile faith is not just about babies. It's about any area where you feel barren or "behind."

- Infertility, pregnancy loss, or the painful discovery that biological children may not be part of your story.
- Choosing adoption, fostering, step-parenting, or spiritual parenting as the way you will mother.
- Career stagnation while others advance.
- Singleness while attending wedding after wedding.
- A business that won't take off.
- A degree that feels like it will never be finished.
- A ministry, calling, or dream that feels stuck in neutral.

Yet, the Hannah principle still applies: Specific requests require specific prayers – with stewardship attached. Hannah didn't just pray, *"Lord, give me a baby."* She prayed, in essence, *"Give me a son, and I will give him back to You."* She attached a give-back plan to her ask.

And to my Black, Caribbean, African American, Latina, and African sisters: statistics show that among premature babies, Black baby girls have some of the highest survival rates. If we can arrive early and still survive, imagine what happens when we reach full term – in the spirit and in life. We are built with the capacity to endure, adapt, and rise. That resilience isn't just cultural; it's spiritual DNA. We are literally built to survive hard starts – so in the spirit, don't be surprised when you outlast things that should've taken you out.

We are some of the most "fertile souls," which often means more manure gets dumped on us. But I declare that God is granting double-portion favor, divine wisdom, and creative strategies – not only from what people hand you, but from what you and God build together.

Sometimes, delay is not denial. It's protection. God knows you better than you know yourself. Like a wise spouse saying, "I'm not going to let you promise that – you don't have the capacity for that right now," God will sometimes hold back an answer to keep you out of trouble with Him and with yourself. Whether your story includes children, adoption, bonus kids, spiritual sons and daughters, or no kids at all, your life can still be wildly fertile in the Kingdom.

Kingdom Strategies for Fertile Faith

1. Transform Your Pain Points

Make a list of your Peninnah moments – the triggers that remind you of what you don't have or what still hurts:

+ A person's comments
+ A social media account that stirs comparison
+ A recurring family question that leaves you feeling "less than"
+ A date on the calendar that reminds you of loss

Not to wallow – but to war strategically. When you can identify where the enemy pokes you, you can aim your prayers like arrows instead of swinging wildly in the dark. Every time Peninnah "shows up" (online, at dinner, in your mind), let that be your cue: This is my prayer assignment.

2. Craft Your Breakthrough Blueprint

Hannah negotiated with heaven. She didn't just ask. She planned: "Lord, if You give me a son, I will give him back to You all his life." God responds to faith with a plan. Write down:

+ Your specific request
+ Your stewardship plan (How will you care for this blessing – whether it's a child, a business, a book, a ministry, or a healed heart?)

+ Your give-back commitment (How will this answer serve God and others?)

Examples:

» "Lord, if You bless me with this promotion, I will mentor three women in my field each year."

» "Lord, if You heal my womb or lead me through adoption, I will raise this child to know You and support other women walking their own fertility or adoption journeys."

» "Lord, if You cause my business to flourish, I will employ single mothers and build a generous giving rhythm into the company."

Don't just ask for the blessing – attach your stewardship to it. God is looking for partners, not just recipients.

3. Pour Sessions: Daily 10-Minute Soul Pour

Hannah poured out her soul before the Lord. The word used in the text conveys the idea of complete emptiness. Set a timer for 10 minutes each day this week. Let it all out:

+ The ugly cry
+ The frustration
+ The questions
+ The hope you're almost afraid to admit

The Holy Spirit interprets your groans when words fail. A transformation happens when you stop stuffing and start pouring. Many times, your face will change – like Hannah's countenance did – before your circumstances do.

Fertile Faith Takeaways

1. **Your barrenness is not your identity.**
   You are still the beloved, even when you're waiting. Hannah was loved before, during, and after her barrenness. So are you – whether or not your story includes children

2. **Specific requests require specific prayers.**
   Vague prayers get vague answers. Hannah asked for a son with a specific plan attached. You can do the same with your own "Samuel prayer" – for a dream, assignment, healing, or direction.

3. **The thing mocking you today can become your ministry tomorrow.**
   God turns pain into purpose, mocking into ministry. On the other side of Hannah's barrenness, a prophet was born who would anoint kings. On the other side of your Peninnah moments, there is someone you will comfort, coach, or lead because you've walked this road.

Fertile Faith Prayer

Lord, Father God:

You see this sister in her fertile faith journey. You know every tear she's cried in secret, every taunt from her Peninnah, every time she's been misunderstood by people who should have comforted her. As You did for Hannah, we ask You to remember her. Take the mockery and recycle it as fertilizer for her future. Take the pain of her past and turn it into a powerful purpose. We speak to her spiritual womb — open in Jesus' name. Call forth the dreams, visions, businesses, books, babies, ministries, assignments, adoptions, and breakthroughs that have been delayed or redirected, but not forgotten by You. We lift before You: Those longing for children. Those grieving miscarriage, stillbirth, or infant loss. Those navigating fertility treatments and hard medical reports. Those walking the path of adoption or fostering. Those raising bonus children and spiritual sons and daughters. Those who have discovered that their story will not include motherhood — and are still called, still worthy, still wildly fruitful in Your Kingdom. Bless their bodies, their minds, their choices, and their journeys. Surround them with wise doctors, safe communities, and Your tender presence. She is bringing You a specific request with a specific plan. She's not just asking to be blessed; she's ready to steward the blessing — whatever it looks like — for Your glory. Thank You that You are working even when Peninnah is loud, and Eli gets it wrong. Transform her tears into testimony. Turn her barrenness into a breakthrough, her empty places into fertile ground. Let her story encourage generations of women who think their waiting season will never end. We declare this is her set time for fertile faith to produce a harvest.

In Jesus' name, Amen.

Fertile Faith Challenge

This week don't just endure your "Peninnah moments" – let God use them as fertilizer for your faith.

1. **Name Your Peninnah (Bring It Out of Hiding)** – Who or what keeps reminding you of what you lack or what still hurts? A person's comments? A social media highlight reel? An environment that makes you feel "behind"? A date, holiday, or anniversary that stirs grief?

   Journal: "My Peninnah right now is ____________ because __________." Naming it helps you stop fighting shadows and start bringing the real issue into the light with God.

2. **Write Your Hannah Prayer (Turn Pain into Petition)** – Set aside 10–15 quiet minutes. Pour it all out – like Hannah. In your journal, write: What does

Peninnah's presence or words stir up in you (jealousy, shame, anger, fear, feeling forgotten, grief)? What do you truly desire from God in this area (be specific)? Include a faith declaration, even if your voice is shaking.

Example starter:
"Lord, You see the sting in my heart when______ _____________ happens. I feel _____________, but by faith I ask You for _____________. Remember me in this place. Don't waste this pain – use it as fertilizer for my future."

Journal: Finish that prayer in your own words. Be raw. God can handle it.

3. **Find Your Fertile Faith Partner (Activate Agreement & Healing)** – Choose one trusted sister – someone who can handle your heart and your hope. Share with her:

   » What your "Peninnah" is.
   » The specific request you're believing in God for?
   » Ask her to pray in agreement with you at least once this week.
   » Ask her to check in (text, call, voice note) to remind you what **God** said – not what Peninnah said.

Journal (after you share): "How did it feel to invite someone into this place? What did God show me through their encouragement or prayer?"

> **Remember:** Hannah's face changed before her womb did. Your breakthrough begins the moment you pour out and partner in faith – not just when you receive.

Tomorrow's Teaser:
Formula Faith with Joseph

Today, we watched a woman turn her pain into a prayer that changed generations. Tomorrow, we'll meet a man who took revelation and turned it into a blueprint that fed nations. If you've ever thought, *"God, I know I'm built for more – but how do I turn all this faith, insight, and information into real steps, real systems, and real security for my family,"* Day 3 is your wake-up call. Success leaves clues. Divine revelation releases downloads. Tomorrow, with Joseph, we're going to lean into both – so you can start building a life that doesn't just *shout* faith but quietly **secures** the future for you and the generations coming behind you.

DAY 3

FORMULA FAITH

Joseph's Strategic Seasons
& The Proverbs 31 Blueprint

Formula (FOR-myuh-lah) – *noun*

+ A mathematical relationship or rule expressed in symbols
+ A list of ingredients with their proportions
+ A method, pattern, or rule for doing or producing something
+ A plan devised for dealing with a specific problem

Kingdom Definition: A God-given blueprint that transforms divine revelation into practical application, turning promise into provision for generations.

Formula Faith Scripture Foundation:
(Primary) Genesis 41:34–3, 47–49, 53–57 (NIV)

34 Let Pharaoh appoint commissioners over the land to take a fifth of the harvest of Egypt during the seven years of abundance. 35 hey should collect all the food of these good years that are coming and store up the grain under the authority of Pharaoh, to be kept in the cities for food. 36 This food should be held in reserve for the country, to be used during the seven years of famine that will come upon Egypt, so that the country may not be ruined by the famine." 47 During the seven years of abundance the land produced plentifully. 48 Joseph collected all the food produced in those seven years of abundance in Egypt and stored it in the cities. In each city he put the food grown in the fields surrounding it. 49 Joseph stored up huge quantities of grain, like the sand of the sea; it was so much that he stopped keeping records because it was beyond measure. 53 The seven years of abundance in Egypt came to an end, 54 and the seven years of famine began, just as Joseph had said. There was famine in all the other lands, but in the whole land of Egypt there was food. 55 When all Egypt began to feel the famine, the people cried to Pharaoh for food. Then Pharaoh told all the Egyptians, "Go to Joseph and do what he tells you." 56 When the famine had spread over the whole country, Joseph opened all the storehouses and sold grain to the Egyptians, for the famine was severe throughout Egypt. 57 And all the world came to Egypt to buy grain from Joseph, because the famine was severe everywhere.

Supporting Scripture: Proverbs 31:15–16, 21, 27

Additional Scripture: Proverbs 6:6–8; Luke 14:28–30

Big Idea: God doesn't just give you vision – He gives you formulas. When you partner His revelation with strategic preparation, your faithful obedience can pre-serve whole families and feed nations in their famine.

The Deep Dive: Joseph's Formula in the Fire

Family, picture this: a 30-year-old former slave and ex-prisoner standing before the most powerful ruler in the world, with a 14-year strategic plan downloaded straight from heaven. Not a suggestion. Not a "maybe," but a formula that would save **nations**.

Yet, Joseph shouldn't even have been in that room. He grew up in a house where dysfunction was the family language. His father Jacob had two wives, Leah and Rachel, and a clear hierarchy. Rachel was the beloved; Leah was the overlooked. Leah kept having babies, trying to earn Jacob's love – *"Now my husband will love me...now he will be attached to me"* – baby after baby, hoping his heart would change.

Rachel, the beloved, was barren until Joseph. When Joseph finally arrived, Jacob's joy overflowed into that famous coat of many colors, flaunted in front of sons who had watched their mother be treated like second best. Resentment was already simmering.

And Joseph? Whew. He didn't help himself. At 17, walking around in his designer coat, he has not one but two dreams in which his brothers – and even his parents – bow to him. And what does this teenage brother do? He tells *all* of them. "Joseph had a dream, and when he told it to his brothers, they hated him all the more" (Genesis 37:5).

Baby, let me tell you something about emotional intelligence and spiritual discretion: **Your revelation is not for everybody's consumption.** Joseph had a real dream from God – but he shared it with the wrong audience in the wrong way at the wrong time. He was gifted but unseasoned. His lack of wisdom poured fuel on a fire that was already burning in that family.

From there, his brothers plotted to kill him, then "settled" for selling him into slavery for twenty pieces of silver – less than the price of a disabled slave. They smeared his coat with blood, handed it to their father, and let him believe his favorite son was dead.

Over time, Joseph's life became one long pit-to-palace journey:

- **Pit:** Thrown in a hole by his own brothers.
- **Potiphar's house:** Sold as a slave, but everything he touches prospers; he ends up running the whole house.
- **Prison:** Falsely accused by Potiphar's wife because he refused to sleep with her. He should've been executed, but instead he's incarcerated – and once again, he ends up running the place.
- **Palace:** Interprets Pharaoh's disturbing dreams and doesn't just give the meaning – he delivers a full-scale implementation strategy.

Everywhere Joseph goes, he makes broken systems better. That's a word all by itself:

> **Formula Faith Principle:** A future-forward believer leaves every place better than they found it – even places meant to break them.

Formula Faith in a Shaky World

By the time Joseph stands before Pharaoh, Egypt is facing a revelation with massive implications:

+ Seven years of prosperity
+ Seven years of famine
+ Zero time machines

Joseph interprets Pharaoh's dream and then immediately lays out a formula: a plan to *buy* the future through wise storage and strategic distribution. For example, if we had known COVID was coming, we all would've done some things differently – including investing our money, time, rest, relationships, and yes, even toilet paper. If we knew exactly when it would end, we would've paced ourselves differently. We don't get exact dates on everything. But we *do* have a God who still gives formulas – Spirit-led strategies that help us prepare in real time for what we can't yet see.

Right now, we live in days of shifting policies, changing economies, and constant headlines that could keep us up at night: student loans, healthcare access, job markets, inflation, and global instability. If you're not rooted, you'll live in fight-or-flight. This is why Joseph's story is a reminder: **When the world is shaking, God is still giving His people formulas.**

Joseph's 20% Principle

Here's the core of Joseph's plan: "*Let Pharaoh appoint commissioners over the land to take a fifth of the harvest of Egypt during the seven years of abundance...This food should be held in reserve...to be used during the seven years of famine*" (Genesis 41:34–36, NIV).

Joseph's formula was simple but powerful:

+ **Seven years of abundance:** Store 20% of everything.
+ **Seven years of famine:** Open the storehouses and distribute strategically.
+ **Result:** Egypt becomes the world's supplier. Nations come to them for food – including Joseph's own family.

Here's a simple way to see that plan as a Kingdom formula – three "equations" you can actually live by:

1. **Revelation + Preparation = Preservation**
   » God revealed what was coming; Joseph prepared accordingly. Together, that partnership *preserved* lives. Revelation is God's part. Preparation is your part. Preservation is the outcome.

2. **Current Surplus ÷ 5 = Future Security**
   » Joseph took one-fifth (20%) of the harvest during the good years. That small, consistent slice created massive stability later. Even a little margin, multiplied over time, becomes protection in a crisis.

3. **Strategic Storage + Systematic Distribution = Generational Provision**
   » Joseph didn't just store grain; he organized it and released it wisely. Saving *plus* structure created provision not only for Egypt, but for surrounding nations and his entire family line.

Formula Faith says: *"What I have now is not just for now. It's a seed for the future – if I treat it like a seed."* For us, that 20% might look like:

- **20% of your income** → emergency savings, investments, or debt payoff
- **20% of your energy** → reserved before you hit burnout
- **20% of your time** → planning, learning, and system-building – not just reacting
- **20% of your resources** → set aside to create margin before a crisis hits

Joseph didn't hoard out of fear. He stored with a strategy.

The Proverbs 31 Blueprint: Daily Execution

Joseph shows us macro strategy – national-level planning. Likewise, the "Proverbs 31 Woman" shows us micro execution: how formula faith looks in everyday life.

"She gets up while it is still night; she provides food for her family and portions for her female servants." (Proverbs 31:15) – That's **strategic scheduling** and **delegation**.

"She considers a field and buys it; out of her earnings she plants a vineyard." (v. 16) – That's **calculated investment**.

"When it snows, she has no fear for her household; for all of them are clothed in scarlet." (v. 21) – That's **winter prep** – she has no fear of the season because she has a formula.

"She watches over the affairs of her household and does not eat the bread of idleness." (v. 27) – That's **active management** instead of passive drifting.

The Proverbs 31 Woman has:
+ A household management formula
+ Delegation systems (assigning tasks to her servants)
+ Diversified income streams (fields, vineyards, trading)

Are you interested in ways you can start applying these concepts? Here are some examples you can begin utilizing now at home:

+ Delivery services and convenience tools that aren't automatically wasteful – if your income is tied to time, outsourcing groceries might *save* you money because it frees you to work.
+ Reward programs (apps, fuel points, dining rewards) are tiny formulas that keep more money in your pocket when you use them intentionally.

In other words:
+ Joseph built formulas for nations.
+ The Proverbs 31 woman ran formulas for households.
+ **You've been called to do both**: village-level strategy *and* daily-life systems.

Kingdom Strategies for Formula Faith

1. **Identify Your Harvest Season**

Not every season is a famine. Proverbs tells us to "consider the ant," who stores in summer what it will need later (Proverbs 6:6–8). Your harvest might look like:
» Overtime checks
» Tax refunds or bonuses
» Extra clients or contracts
» "Random" direct deposit blessings or surprise checks

The Proverbs 31 woman "sees that her trading is profitable" (v. 18). She notices when things are up. Joseph did the same in Egypt – he recognized the seven years of plenty and treated them as *preparation time*, not a permanent lifestyle.

Sometimes, harvest shows up as barter: You may have traded design and branding skills for your daughters' hair to be done. You may have built a school website in exchange for your child's tuition. These action items are considered harvest too.

> **Formula Faith Move:** Ask yourself, *"What is my harvest in this season?"* Then decide what percentage you will **store**, not spend.

2. **Design Your Daily Formula (Not Just Wishes)**

Wishing things were different is not the same as building a different way of doing life. Joseph didn't just say, "We should probably save some grain." He created:

» Collection points

» Storage cities

» Distribution channels

The Proverbs 31 woman doesn't just "hope" her household will run smoothly. She has:

» Supplier relationships

» Production systems

» Market presence

» Delegation rhythms

Here are other examples of modern formulas:

» Automatic transfers for savings and giving
» Proposal templates so clients get offers within 24 hours
» CRMs or simple workflows that generate contracts and invoices with one click

Alternatively, we lose so much time and money not because we're lazy, but because we're unsystematic.

Formula Faith Principle: A system is just a repeated way of solving the same problem on purpose. Where do you need a formula?

» Money (budgets, auto-saving, rewards)
» Meals (meal plans, grocery lists, rotating menus)
» Mornings (routines that center you instead of adding chaos)
» Clients (onboarding, proposals, follow-up)
» Home (laundry rhythms, kids' chores, bill-payment dates)

Don't just *wish* things would change. Design one small daily formula that starts the change.

3. **Prepare for Other People's Famine**

Joseph's preparation didn't just bless Egypt – it became the distribution center for surrounding nations. His formula faith literally fed the very brothers who betrayed him. Even right now, when systems like SNAP get disrupted, food banks feel the impact for months. When famines hit – economic, emotional, or spiritual – someone must be ready.

The Proverbs 31 woman "opens her arms to the poor" (v. 20). She is personally generous because she is structurally prepared. In the same way, your overflow can become:

» Groceries for a neighbor
» Gas money for a single mom
» A scholarship for a child
» A pro bono strategy call for someone in crisis

Your *daily bread* seasons are different from your *overflow* seasons – you learned this from your father. Manna came day by day; sometimes, that "the bill shows up when the client pays" rhythm is God's way of sustaining you. But when overflow *does* come, Formula Faith asks: *"Who else am I supposed to feed?"* Formula Faith isn't about hoarding. It's about **holy administration**.

Formula Faith Takeaways

1. **God doesn't just give visions; He gives strategies.** Joseph didn't only interpret dreams; he implemented systems. Revelation without preparation leaves people hungry.

2. **Your formula is often hidden in your frustration.** That recurring problem you can't stop noticing? That "unique agitation" is often a clue to the problem you're designed to solve. You are the *formula fixer* for that thing.

3. **Excellence in every season prepares you for elevation.** Joseph excelled in Potiphar's house, in prison, and in the palace. Before he managed a nation's grain, he managed another man's house. Before he ran a distribution center, he ran a jail. Your "little" assignments are training for your "Egypt" one day.

Formula Faith Prayer

Lord,

Thank You for being a God of order and not chaos. Just as You gave Joseph a formula for nations and the Proverbs 31 woman a blueprint for her household, I ask You to download my divine strategy. Please show me my 20%. Reveal what I need to store, when to distribute, and how to systematize Your blessing. Turn my survival mode into strategic mode. Help me recognize that my pits have been preparation – not punishment.

Like Joseph, give me the grace to forgive those who hurt me and the wisdom to build systems that will one day even bless them. Give me Formula Faith that outlasts any famine. Teach me to steward my harvest, create godly systems, and prepare not just for my own needs, but for the needs of my village. Make me a trustworthy treasurer of Your resources.

In Jesus' mighty name, Amen.

Formula Faith Challenge

This week, we're not just shouting about breakthrough – we're building formulas.

1. **Map Your 20%** – Pick **one** area: money, time, or energy.

    » **Money:** Look at your last month's income. What would 20% look like as savings, debt payoff, or investment?

    » **Time:** How could you reserve 20% of your week for planning, learning, and rest *before* burnout?

    » **Energy:** Where can you stop overspending yourself so you have margin for what matters?

    Journal: "What is my 20% in this season? What small, consistent action will I start this week to protect it?"

2. **Identify Your Joseph Journey** – Look back over your life:

    » Who (or what) was your "pit"?

    » Where did you learn to lead in places that were supposed to break you – like Joseph in Potiphar's house or in prison?

    » What skills, character traits, or spiritual muscles did you gain there that you're using now?

    Journal: "My pit prepared me to ______________. In that season, I learned ______________, which now helps me ______________."

Let the Holy Spirit show you that your detours were actually designed to guide you to your purpose.

3. **Build One Simple System** – Choose one area of chaos and create a basic formula:

   » A meal-planning blueprint (for example, themed nights: pasta Monday, taco Tuesday, soup Wednesday)

   » A client process (consult → proposal within 24 hours → contract → invoice)

   » A money system (auto-transfer on payday + rewards points plan)

   » A household rhythm (shared family calendar + weekly check-in)

   Journal: "What system did I build? What problem does it solve? How will I keep it going (automation, reminders, delegation)?"

Remember: Joseph's coat made him a target, but his character and systems made him a treasurer. His brothers meant to enslave him for evil, but God meant it for good. God used Joseph's formula of faith to feed the very people who once rejected him. Your purpose is deeply connected to the formulas you're divinely created to fix. So, let's get to it!

Tomorrow's Teaser:
Fireproof Faith with the Three Hebrew Boys

Joseph shows us how to plan through seasons of abundance and famine. Tomorrow, we step into the furnace with three Hebrew boys whose convictions were so fixed that even a fire turned seven times hotter couldn't make them bow. Get ready for **Fireproof Faith** – where your loyalty to God gets tested by the flames, but what was meant to consume you becomes the very stage where His power is put on display.

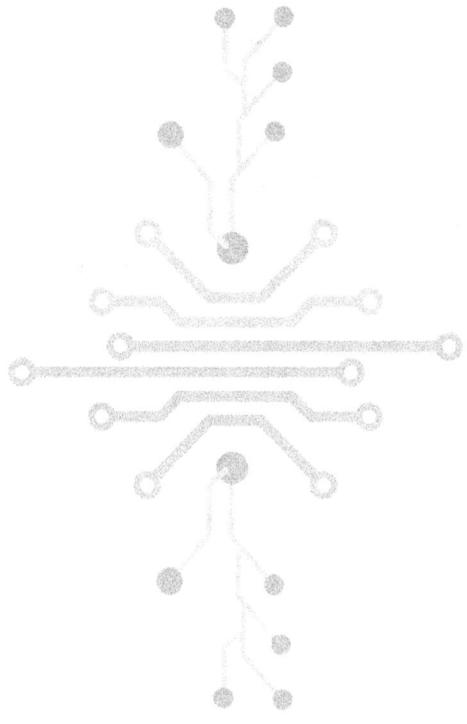

DAY 4

FIREPROOF FAITH

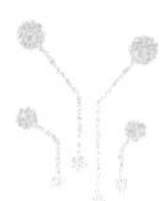

When the Heat Gets Turned Up
Seven Times Hotter

Fireproof (ˈfī(ə)rˌpro͞of) – *adjective*

- ✦ Resistant to destruction by fire
- ✦ Able to withstand intense heat without burning
- ✦ Protected against fire damage
- ✦ Impervious to flames

Kingdom Definition: Faith that remains uncompromised under extreme pressure; refuses to bow to false gods, and emerges from the furnace without even the smell of smoke.

Fireproof Faith Scripture Foundation:
(Primary) Daniel 3:16–18, 24–27 (ESV)

16 Shadrach, Meshach, and Abednego answered and said to the king, "O Nebuchadnezzar, we have no need to answer you in this matter. 17 If this be so, our God whom we serve is able to deliver us from the burning fiery furnace, and he will deliver us out of your hand, O king. 18 But if not, be it known to you, O king, that we will not serve your gods or worship the golden image that you have set up."

"24 Then King Nebuchadnezzar was astonished and rose up in haste. He declared to his counselors, "Did we not cast three men bound into the fire?" They answered and said to the king, "True, O king." 25 He answered and said, "But I see four men unbound, walking in the midst of the fire, and they are not hurt; and the appearance of the fourth is like a son of the gods." 26 Then Nebuchadnezzar came near to the door of the burning fiery furnace; he declared, "Shadrach, Meshach, and Abednego, servants of the Most High God, come out, and come here!" Then Shadrach, Meshach, and Abednego came out from the fire. 27 And the satraps, the prefects, the governors, and the king's counselors gathered together and saw that the fire had not had any power over the bodies of those men. The hair of their heads was not singed, their cloaks were not harmed, and no smell of fire had come upon them.

Supporting Scripture: Isaiah 43:2; 1 Peter 1:7; James 1:2–4
Additional Scripture: Hebrews 11:34; Malachi 3:3

> **Big Idea:** Fireproof faith doesn't just believe God *can* deliver – it refuses to bow even if He doesn't, trusting that the same fire meant to consume you will become the setting for your testimony and promotion.

The Deep Dive:
Three Boys, Seven-Fold Heat, and the "No Smoke" Testimony

Family, one of my favorite things to say when people tell me, "You don't look like a grandma," or "You don't look your age," is: "*Girl, I don't look like what I've been through.*" That's exactly the kind of energy we see with Shadrach, Meshach, and Abednego. These Hebrew boys were thrown into a furnace turned up seven times hotter than normal, and walked out without even *smelling* like smoke. But to appreciate that miracle, we need to see the setup.

King Nebuchadnezzar – listen, we really could do a whole micro-study on this brother – had issues. He loved being worshiped. He loved being praised. He surrounded himself with yes-men who only told him what he wanted to hear. Sound familiar? How many of us have worked for leaders who:

+ Need constant admiration
+ Can't handle disagreement
+ Treat every "no" like a personal attack

Similarly, Nebuchadnezzar builds a golden statue – ninety feet high, nine feet wide – and issues a decree: when the music plays, *everybody* bows. No exceptions. No religious exemptions. No, "I'll just stand quietly in the back." Bow or burn. Period. Well, Shadrach, Meshach, and Abednego decide they're not doing it. There is one true and living God, and they refuse to bend the knee to a counterfeit.

The Setup: When Haters Become Informants

Daniel 3:8 says, *"At this time some astrologers came forward and denounced the Jews."* Translation: the haters could not wait to snitch. Think about workplace bullies or messy folks at church, and how they react when:

+ You're doing your work with excellence.
+ You're minding your business.
+ You're living in your purpose.

Here come the people who stay in everybody's business (but their own), running to the boss like kids tattling to mama:

+ *"They're disrespecting you."*
+ *"They're making you look bad."*
+ *"They said you're not going to do anything about it."*

> **Understand this:** When you take a stand for God, people who are comfortable bowing will put a bullseye on you. The astrologers didn't just report facts – they hyped the situation to make sure these boys caught maximum heat.

The Confrontation:
The Birthplace of Fireproof Faith

Verse 13 says Nebuchadnezzar was *"furious with rage."* Not just annoyed. Not just offended. **FURIOUS. WITH. RAGE.** When your faith challenges someone's ego, expect the temperature to rise. As a result, the king drags the three Hebrew boys in and basically says, *Is it true? Are y'all really defying my order? I'll give you one more chance. Bow when the music plays – or burn.* That's the pre-furnace moment – where everything in you is tempted to compromise "just a little" to keep the peace, keep the job, or keep the relationship.

But this is where Fireproof Faith is born. Their answer is legendary: *"King Nebuchadnezzar, we do not need to defend ourselves before you in this matter. If we are thrown into the blazing furnace, the God we serve is able to deliver us from it, and he will deliver us from Your Majesty's hand. But even if he does not, we want you to know, Your Majesty, that we will not serve your gods or worship the image of gold you have set up"* (Daniel 3:16–18, NIV).

The Three-Part Declaration of Fireproof Faith

Let's break down their formula – because this is **your** blueprint:

Part 1: "The God we serve is able to deliver us…"

They start with God's *ability*, not their *eligibility*. Some of you are stuck on the wrong question: *"Do I deserve to be delivered?"* That's not the issue. The real question is: **"Is God able?"** Empty tomb says yes. Every miracle you've ever seen says yes. The fact that you're still here says yes. Fireproof Faith starts by anchoring itself in who God *is* – not in how worthy you feel.

Part 2: "…and He will deliver us…"

Now, we are moving on from theology to expectation. Not *"maybe* He will." Not "we *hope* so." This is a prophetic declaration – calling things that are not as though they were, talking themselves out of the furnace *before* they ever hit the flames. They don't know *how* He will do it. They don't know *when* He will do it. But they are fully persuaded: "Our God is not just able in general – He will move on *our* behalf." That's not arrogance; that's covenant confidence.

Part 3: "But even if He does not…"

This is where Fireproof Faith goes from cute to costly. This line separates ***real faith*** from fair-weather faith. "Even if I don't get the outcome I want, I still won't bow." Even if I lose the job, even if the diagnosis doesn't change, even if the relationship ends, even if the promotion goes to somebody else, **I still won't betray my God.** This is the heartbeat of Fireproof Faith: "My obedience is not up for negotiation – no matter how hot the furnace gets."

The Furnace: Seven Times Hotter

The king snaps. He orders the furnace heated seven times hotter than usual. Seven is the number of completion. The enemy often tries to "completely" destroy you when you refuse to compromise. It gets so hot that the soldiers who throw the boys into the fire die from the heat. Let that sink in: God will keep you in situations that the people standing right next to you cannot stand. They can't stand the pain. They can't stand the process.

They fold under the same pressure that God sustains you through. The difference is not that you're better than them; the difference is that your faith is anchored in someone greater than you.

The Fourth Man:
You Are Not Alone in This Fire

Then we hit verse 25, and it gets supernatural: "Look! I see four men walking around in the fire, unbound and unharmed, and the fourth looks like a son of the gods." (Daniel 3:25)

That fourth man is a pre-incarnate appearance of Jesus – showing up in the Old Testament furnace before Bethlehem, before Calvary, before the empty tomb.

That promise, *"I will never leave you nor forsake you,"* is not a cute refrigerator magnet.

It's a **furnace promise**. God will show up:

+ In the HR meeting
+ In the chemo ward
+ In the courtroom
+ In the late-night tears

You do not have to go through the fire alone.

The Testimony:
No Smoke. No Smell. Just Glory!

When Nebuchadnezzar calls them out, verse 27 says: "The fire had not harmed their bodies, nor was a hair of their heads singed; their robes were not scorched, and there was **no smell of fire** on them." Therefore, I speak this over you: This trial you're in – this fiery season, this furnace you're walking through – you are coming out of it **without a hint of smoke on you**. You will not look like what you've been through. You will not smell like what you've been through. People will look at you and say, "How did you survive *that* and still have your joy, your mind, your faith?" That's Fireproof Faith.

Real-Life Fireproof Faith: When Conviction Costs You

Let's bring this down to real life. I remember being in an executive role where staff were being mistreated. I spoke up. My husband has a similar story. In both cases, here's what we learned:

+ Before the furnace: everybody's cheering. "Say something! Stand up! We're with you!"
+ When the heat gets turned up: silence.

Because at the end of the day, people want change, at somebody else's expense. As a result, I lost that position, and I lost that job. But God had me land on my feet – with:

+ More money
+ Better benefits
+ The ability to take care of my family in ways I couldn't before

One specific area? Insurance. My former company wasn't willing to honor what they'd promised. God moved me into a situation where that need was not just met – it was exceeded.

That's Fireproof Faith: You might lose the position, but you keep your soul – and gain God's provision.

We've also seen public leaders (regardless of your views on them) who stood ten toes down on their convictions. They were criticized, campaigned against, written off – and yet, later, they're in rooms with former critics smiling in their faces. Not because they bowed, but because they didn't. The lesson? You don't have to bow to be used by God. He can position you to serve and influence without compromise.

To my **after-5 CEOs** – those of you with day jobs and kingdom assignments after hours:

+ Your workplace furnace might be blazing because you refuse to join the gossip.
+ Your business furnace might be hot because you won't lie on reports or adopt "everybody does it" shortcuts.

Your greatest currency in God's kingdom is faithfulness and character. Trust Him with the rest.

The Warning:
Don't Let Fear Make You Bow

Some of you are one furnace away from promotion, but fear has you considering compromise. You're thinking:

+ "Maybe I'll bow just a little…"
+ "Just enough to keep the job…"
+ "Just enough to keep the peace…"

But hear me: **Partial bowing is still bowing.** You can't bow to idols Monday through Friday and then try to stand for God on Sunday. Your Fireproof Faith must work:

+ In the boardroom
+ In the group chat
+ In your relationship
+ In the prayer room

The Promise:
Promotion After the Fire

Daniel 3:30 says, "Then the king promoted Shadrach, Meshach, and Abednego in the province of Babylon." They were promoted *after* the fire – **because** of how they stood in it.

That furnace:

+ Didn't finish them – it *refined* them.
+ Didn't bury them – it *boosted* them.
+ Didn't cancel them – it *commissioned* them.

That betrayal that's trying to break you? It's positioning you for a breakthrough. That rejection that's trying to wreck you? It's redirecting you to your assignment. That furnace that is trying to finish you? It's preparing you for your future.

Kingdom Strategies for Fireproof Faith

1. **Rehearse Your Refusal to Bow**

   Before you get to the furnace, decide what you *will not* bow to:

   » Compromised integrity
   » Idolatry of money, status, or people
   » Abusive leadership or toxic culture
   » Patterns that dishonor God in your body, business, or relationships

Journal: Where are you being pressured to bow? What does obedience to God actually look like in this situation? Then write your own version of their declaration: *"My God is able to deliver me from _______________. I believe He will deliver me. But even if He doesn't, I still will not bow to _______________."* Read it out loud until your spirit believes what your mouth is saying.

2. **Locate Your Fourth-Man Moments**

Think back over your life: When were you in a "furnace" that should've broken you? Who walked away or gave up when you kept standing? Where did you sense God's presence carrying you in ways you couldn't explain?

Journal: What are your 'fourth man' moments? How did God show up in the fire with you – emotionally, financially, spiritually, practically? Naming those moments now strengthens your faith for the furnace you're in.

3. **Stand in Public, Not Just in Private**

Your greatest witness is not always your words – it's your walk-through. Shadrach, Meshach, and Abednego didn't hold a press conference. They simply refused to bow. Their convictions converted a king.

Journal: Where is God asking you to take a *visible* stand? What might it cost you? What might it reveal about Him? Ask God for the courage to stand – not just to post, vent, or complain.

Fireproof Faith Takeaways

1. **Your conviction intimidates their compromise.** That's why some people are so pressed. Your very existence exposes what they're willing to bow to. **Some encounters with God only happen in furnaces.** The fourth man shows up *in* the fire. You will know God in ways you never could have if everything stayed room temperature.

2. **Your survival will convert some of your critics.** Nebuchadnezzar ultimately acknowledged their God as the true God and forbade anyone to speak against Him. Your fireproof testimony will make people re-evaluate the God you serve.

Fireproof Faith Prayer

Lord,

I thank You for being the fourth man in my furnace. When my enemies turn up the heat seven times hotter, You turn up Your presence seven times stronger. Give me Fireproof Faith that refuses to bow, refuses to bend, refuses to break. Please help me understand that not smelling like smoke is part of my testimony. Not looking like what I've been through is part of my witness. Standing when others fall is part of my ministry. I declare that I will not bow to the golden statues of this world – not for position, not for provision, not for people. My God is able to deliver me. I believe He will deliver me. But even if He does not, I still won't bow.

In Jesus' name, Amen.

Fireproof Faith Challenge

This week, don't just read about fireproof faith – practice it.

1. **Name Your Furnace** – Where is the heat being turned up in your life? Work? Family? Finances? Health? Ministry?

   Journal: *"My current furnace is _______________. The pressure I feel is _______________."* Being specific helps you stop feeling vaguely overwhelmed and start fighting strategically.

2. **Write Your "Even If" Declaration** – Complete this sentence in your own words: *"Even if God doesn't _______________, I still will not _______________."* Maybe: *"Even if God doesn't move me from this job as fast as I want, I still will not lie on my reports." "Even if God doesn't restore this relationship, I still will not go back to old toxic patterns." "Even if God doesn't open that door yet, I still will not manipulate my way in."*

   Journal: Write it, date it, and read it out loud once a day this week.

3. **Prophesy Your "No Smoke" Testimony** – Look at your furnace and answer these by faith: What will "not smelling like smoke" look like in my situation? What kind of promotion (spiritual, emotional, relational, financial, positional) could be on the other side of this fire?

Journal: *"When I come out of this, I believe I will _______________. My testimony will help _______________ see God differently."*

> **Remember:** You're not going through the fire to be consumed; you're going through to be refined. The same fire that threatened to destroy you is revealing the fourth man walking with you – and your Fireproof Faith is about to become somebody else's salvation testimony.

Tomorrow's Teaser:
Forward Faith with Jabez

Tomorrow, we're moving into **Forward Faith** with Jabez – the man who dared to pray a dangerous, future-shaping prayer that expanded his territory beyond his painful beginning.

Get ready to lean into a bold, simple prayer that moves heaven and makes hell nervous. Your enlargement is about to upset somebody's ecosystem – and position you for a future only faith could have seen coming.

FORWARD FAITH

When Your Name Means "Pain," but Your Prayer Invites Provision

Forward (FOR-werd) – *adjective & adverb*

+ Toward the front, in the direction one is facing
+ Onward in time, place, or order; ahead
+ Moving progressively toward a better state
+ Bold, direct, or unapologetic in manner

Kingdom Definition: Faith that refuses to wear yesterday's pain as your name and dares to pray bold, forward-moving prayers that pull you into everything God has promised.

Forward Faith Scripture Foundation:
(Primary) 1 Chronicles 4:9–10, The Voice

⁹ Jabez, whose name commemorates his mother's labor pains, was more honorable than his brothers. ¹⁰ He asked the God of Israel, "Please bless me and extend my territory. Let Your hand be with me and guard me from harm so I will not experience pain as my mother did." And God did just that.

Supporting Scripture: Luke 11:9–10; Matthew 7:7–8; James 4:2–3, The Voice

Additional Scripture: Proverbs 18:21; Isaiah 43:1; Philippians 3:13–14, The Voice

> **Big Idea:** Forward Faith refuses to let a painful beginning define the size or direction of your life. It asks God boldly to bless, expand, guide, and protect you – and breaks the cycles that named you.

The Deep Dive:
Don't Get Comfortable in Chaos

It is very easy to get caught up in pain, chaos, and trauma that don't even belong to you. Family drama. Church drama. Workplace drama. Relationship drama. If you are not careful, you can end up as a permanent resident in someone else's emotional earthquake.

I will never forget my sister-in-law looking me dead in the face during a season when a relationship in my life was going completely off the rails. I was deteriorating – physically, emotionally, spiritually – trying to keep everything together. She listened, looked at me, and said one sentence I have never forgotten: **"Don't get comfortable in chaos."** *Whew.*

It's one thing to live through a storm. It's another thing to start decorating the storm – setting out throw pillows, hanging curtains, and calling it home. Some of us have built entire personalities, patterns, and identities around chaos:

- You became the fixer in your family, always cleaning up messes you didn't make.
- You stayed in relationships that were draining you because you felt responsible for the other person's healing.
- You absorbed your parents' unhealed trauma until it felt like your own.
- You kept showing up for people who were committed to behaving badly – and then felt guilty for being tired.

It is possible to get so used to walking on eggshells that stillness feels strange. Peace feels suspicious. Stability feels unsafe.

Here's the truth I've learned the hard way: You have to **choose freedom**, and that choice sometimes looks like isolation. Not isolation as in "I don't need anybody," but isolation as in:

- I can't keep letting *you* be the loudest voice in my life.
- I can't keep letting your pain decide my entire personality.
- I can't keep letting your chaos become my cage.

Over time, I realized: **Isolation is often an ingredient in the recipe for acceleration, promotion, and elevation.** God will pull you away so He can pull you forward. He will separate you to save you. He will rearrange people's access to you so they can't keep draining you like "energy vampires" or, in this case, **destiny vampires**. Jabez understood this deeply.

When Someone Else's Pain Names You

Look at how Scripture introduces him: "Jabez, whose name commemorates his mother's labor pains, was more honorable than his brothers" (1 Chronicles 4:9, VOICE). The Amplified Bible version says his mother named him Jabez – *"sorrow-maker"* – because she bore him in pain. His whole identity was stamped with somebody else's trauma.

Every time someone called his name, they were re-announcing her worst day:

"Hey, Pain!"

"Come here, Sorrow."

"Trouble-maker, dinner's ready."

He became a walking memorial to what *she* had lived through. It would be like having a ten-pound baby and naming that child "Ten Pounds" so nobody ever forgets what they put you through.

Recently, I ran across a story from an OB-GYN who treated a woman who had been in constant pelvic pain for twenty-seven years after childbirth. *Twenty-seven years*! Her child's father moved on – remarried, had more children, built a new life – while she stayed stuck in pain from that one delivery.

Eventually, the doctor discovered the problem: a severe tear during childbirth had been stitched in a way that trapped infection in her body. One surgery later, she walked out pain-free for the first time in almost three decades. The physician made a powerful point: The birth changed both of their lives, but only one of them had to live every day with the pain.

Now imagine if she had named that child "Stabbing Pain" or "Bed Bound" – so that every time she looked at him, her trauma was reinforced. That's what happened to Jabez. His mother commemorated her pain more than she celebrated her son. She named him after what she went through.

And still, Scripture says: "Jabez was more honorable than his brothers." The child she named after pain turned out better than the ones she presumably gave "normal" names.

Forward Faith Lesson

What you were **called** is not the same as what you're **called to**. Some of you know exactly what it is to be named after somebody else's brokenness:

+ "You're just like your daddy."
+ "You're too much."
+ "You're hard to love."
+ "You're always the problem."

Or you've internalized the chaos around you so long that the soundtrack of your life has become:

"I am what I survived." Forward Faith says, "I am **not** what hurt me. I am **not** what they call me. I am what God is calling me *into*."

The Short, Powerful Prayer
That Changes Everything

Here's the power move: Jabez did not spend his life trying to convince his mother to rename him. He didn't beg the people around him to see him differently. He took his case **to God**. He asked the God of Israel, *"Please bless me and extend my territory. Let Your hand be with me and guard me from harm so I will not experience pain as my mother did."* And God did just that (1 Chronicles 4:10).

He could have allowed his mother's pain to be his entire life. Instead, he prayed one of the shortest, most effective, forward-moving prayers in the Bible. He didn't pray backward: "Fix my name, fix my image, fix their opinion." He didn't pray stuck: "Help me manage being the sorrow-maker." He prayed **forward**:

+ Bless me.
+ Expand me.
+ Go with me.
+ Break this cycle of pain.

Four lines. One bold prayer. One destiny shifted. Let's unpack each part.

1. "Please bless me."

Not "bless me if I deserve it." Not "bless me when I've finally proved myself." Just:

"Bless. Me." We will bless strangers when they sneeze, but struggle to ask God to bless us on purpose. In your house, if somebody sneezes and nobody says "Bless you," it's an issue. Your husband will literally "achoo" again to remind you to bless him. It's automatic now – you even bless people you don't know. God is inviting you to that same certainty with Him.

Here is your Forward Faith affirmation – the one that belongs on shirts, hoodies, mugs, wallpapers, and deep in your spirit:

The Forward Faith "Bless Me" Declaration

God bless me indeed.
God bless me extremely.
God bless me exceedingly.
God bless me exceptionally.
God bless me especially.
God bless me extraordinarily.
God bless me in the extreme.
God bless me extra.
God bless me tremendously.
God bless me immensely.
God bless me singularly.
God bless me significantly.
God bless me distinctly.
God bless me outstandingly.
God bless me uncommonly.
God bless me unusually.
God bless me supremely.
God bless me highly.
God bless me remarkably.
God bless me thoroughly.
God bless me to a great extent.
God bless me most.

Is it extra? Absolutely. But before you fully yielded to God, you were extra in other directions – extra in sin, extra in rebellion, extra in over-giving to people who didn't value it. Now you've just decided to go that hard for God and for the people assigned to your voice.

If you could be loud in disobedience, you can be loud in obedience.

You're asking God for more wisdom, more wealth, more influence – not just to stunt, but so your cup can overflow *without* you ending up empty. Self-sacrifice is not supposed to leave you with nothing; it's supposed to flow from overflow. Forward Faith says: **"If I'm going hard for them, I'm asking God to go hard for me."**

2. "Extend my territory."

Jabez doesn't just want a blessing. He wants expansion – capacity, reach, and responsibility that match his calling. We are in a season of open doors and endless opportunities. The real test is not whether you'll have options – it's whether you'll have discernment. You've seen this in your own life: At one point, you had multiple opportunities in front of you.

+ **Opportunity A:** Helping develop churches with fresh strategies for changing times. That felt like a green light.
+ **Opportunity B:** Serving in an MLM that looked like it could triple your current income. On paper, it was attractive – but in your spirit, it was a hard red light. You had to say "no" three separate times before they backed off.

Lesson: The enemy can be just as persistent in pushing his will for your life as God is in revealing His, if you're not listening. To my after-5 CEOs and multi-tasking mamas: you're still "paying the mom tax." Your career path wasn't conventional. You chose roles that let you show up for your kids. You went hard for the church as long as you could. If they had wanted your gifts as much as you wanted to give them, you might still be there – but they didn't, and God redirected you. Rejection is not just God's protection – it's His *redirection*. Forward Faith asks God to **extend territory** and then trusts Him when He shuts certain doors along the way.

3. "Let Your hand be with me."

Jabez knows: more territory without God's hand is just more pressure. More visibility = more warfare. More income = more stewardship. He's praying, *Lord, don't just give me more – **go with me** into the more*. This lines up with what many of us are sensing spiritually – a kind of "Year of Yes" for God's people.

+ "Yes" to buildings and houses
+ "Yes" to jobs and businesses
+ "Yes" to opportunities, scholarships, loan deferrals, and forgiveness

But there's a Forward Faith formula attached to that "yes."

+ **OBEY** – Do what God says, when He says it.
+ **PRAY** – Not just emergency prayers – strategic, specific, forward prayers.

+ **STUDY** – Your field, your Bible, your assignment. God will drop supernatural strategies and surreal clarity as you discipline yourself to learn.
+ **GIVE / SOW** – The first fruit of your increase – to your church, to nonprofits, to those in need.
+ **SERVE** – Somewhere. Serving sets you up for supernatural favor.

> Territory + God's hand + obedience = sustained success.

4. "Guard me from harm so I will not experience pain."

This is where Jabez becomes a generational chain-breaker. He is essentially saying: "The pain stops with me. I refuse to let what wounded my mother define my whole life. I will not perpetuate what produced me." Many of us come from generational patterns of pain-naming:

+ Grandmama spoke out of her wounds.
+ Mama carried that forward.
+ If you're not careful, you'll hand the exact same script to your children.

Forward Faith says, **"It stops here."**

And to the one shrinking back because "the market is oversaturated" and "everybody is already doing what I want to do," God has already been preaching down the grocery store aisles. Every time you walk the bread aisle, there's a brand you've never seen. Every time you hit the water aisle, there's a new bottle on the shelf. God's word to you is this: "I gave them a message, but I didn't give them *your* voice. I didn't give them *your* humor. I didn't give them *your* vantage point." You are:

+ A mom and a grandma
+ Caring for kids and aging parents in different stages
+ Managing prolonged hospitalizations, stubborn parents who won't slow down, and loved ones still grieving

And in the middle of all that, He's teaching you about rest, self-care, and wellness – and telling you not to shrink back just because other people got to the topic first. Some people are having a **moment**. You've been called to build a **movement**. Don't let what you were called (by people) keep you from what you're called to (by God).

Kingdom Strategies & Journal Prompts for Forward Faith

1. **Stop Answering to *Old* Names**

   You may not be named "Jabez," but you've been called some things: "Too much." "Needy." "Difficult." "Lazy." "Problem." "Sorrow."

   Journal: What painful name (spoken or implied) have you been answering to? Who gave it to you – family, ex, boss, church, your own inner critic? Now write this confession: *"My name is not my pain. My identity is not my history. My future is not limited by what they call me."*

2. Pray Audaciously Forward

Forward Faith requires **forward** prayers – not just backward processing.

Journal: What territory expansion are you believing for (business, ministry, finances, education, healing, influence)? Where do you need God's hand specifically – wisdom, protection, favor, strategy, stamina? What pain cycle stops with you? Now write a Jabez-style forward prayer that's so bold it makes you a little nervous. Then pray the "God bless me…" declaration out loud once a day this week as your Forward Faith anthem.

3. Document Your Forward Movement

Forward Faith is not just a feeling – it's a movement.

Journal: What opportunities are in front of you right now? List them. Which ones feel like green lights? Which ones feel like red lights, even if they look good on paper? What *one* step can you take this week that clearly moves you toward what God is calling you to – not just away from what hurt you? End with this question: *"A year from now, if I stay in Forward Faith, what will I be moving **toward**, not just recovering **from**?"*

Forward Faith Takeaways

1. **Your painful beginning is not your promised ending.** Jabez went from "sorrow-maker" to history-maker. Your family story is context, not a cage.

2. **Audacious prayers get God's attention.** He didn't pray small because his name was small. He prayed big because his God was big.

3. **Forward Faith requires forward prayers.** At some point, you must stop only praying about what *was* and start boldly praying about what *will be*.

Forward Faith Prayer

Lord,

Like Jabez, I come to You with a painful past but a powerful prayer. I refuse to be defined by what others call me, how I came into this world, or what I cost somebody else. Bless me indeed — extraordinarily, exceptionally, supremely. Enlarge my territory, but keep Your hand on me. Guard me from harm so I will not reproduce the pain that produced me. Let the cycles of sorrow and smallness stop with me. Give me wisdom to know which opportunities are divine and which are distractions. Help me obey while I'm waiting, pray while I'm building, study while I'm stretching, give while I'm growing, and serve while I'm being sharpened. I declare that my name is not my pain. My identity is not my history. My future is not limited by my past. By Your grace, I am moving FORWARD in faith.

In Jesus' name, Amen.

Forward Faith Challenge

This week, implement Forward Faith in a tangible way:

Speak It – Pray the "God bless me" declaration out loud once a day. Let your mouth agree with where God is taking you, not just where you've been.

Write It – Craft your own Jabez prayer and put it somewhere visible (mirror, dashboard, journal, phone wallpaper). Make it short, specific, and forward-focused.

Walk It – Take one concrete step that aligns with the territory you're asking God to expand – send the email, research the program, make the appointment, apply for the opportunity.

> **Remember:**
> + Pain will not define you.
> + The rejection from your top school choice, the betrayal of a romantic partner, the wound of an emotionally unavailable parent, the disappointment of being passed over, the grief of losing someone you love, the church hurt, the layoff, the failure that still stings – none of that is your name.

You are who God says you are. He says you're blessed, your territory is expanding, His hand is on you, and He's guarding you from repeating old pain. Your Forward Faith is about to take you places your family name never could.

Tomorrow's Teaser:
Full Speed Faith with Deborah

Tomorrow, we step into **Full Speed Faith** with Deborah – judge, prophetess, and strategist – who shows us what happens when a woman operates at full kingdom capacity without apology. Get ready to accelerate past your comfort zone and into your calling.

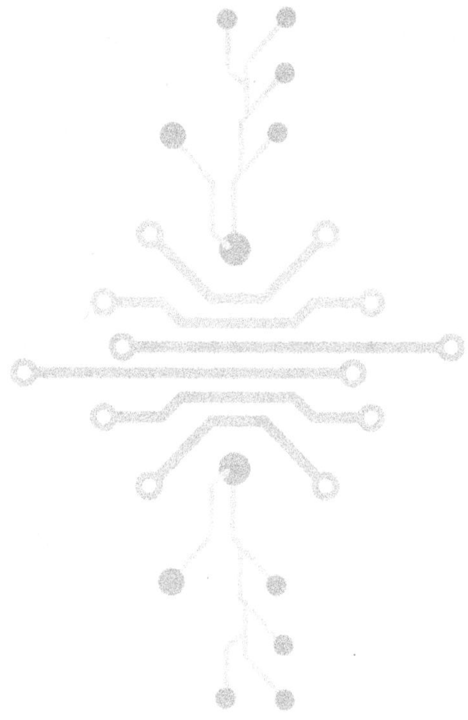

DAY 6
FULL SPEED FAITH

When the Green Light Means **GO!**

Full Speed (fo͞ol-spēd) – *adverb & adjective*
+ Moving at the greatest possible rate; maximum velocity
+ With all engines running at maximum capacity
+ Without hesitation, delay, or reservation
+ Fully committed to forward progress

Kingdom Definition: Faith that responds immediately to God's green light, refusing to sit paralyzed at the intersection of promise and purpose while others honk impatiently behind you and opportunities pass you by.

Full Speed Faith Scripture Foundation: (Primary) Judges 4:4–9, 14–16 (NIV)

4 Now Deborah, a prophet, the wife of Lappidoth, was leading Israel at that time. 5 She held court under the Palm of Deborah between Ramah and Bethel in the hill country of Ephraim, and the Israelites went up to her to have their disputes decided. 6 She sent for Barak son of Abinoam from Kedesh in Naphtali and said to him, "The Lord, the God of Israel, commands you: 'Go, take with you ten thousand men of Naphtali and Zebulun and lead them up to Mount Tabor. 7 I will lead Sisera, the commander of Jabin's army, with his chariots and his troops to the Kishon River and give him into your hands.'" 8 Barak said to her, "If you go with me, I will go; but if you don't go with me, I won't go." 9 "Certainly I will go with you," said Deborah. "But because of the course you are taking, the honor will not be yours, for the Lord will deliver Sisera into the hands of a woman." So Deborah went with Barak to Kedesh.

14 Then Deborah said to Barak, "Go! This is the day the Lord has given Sisera into your hands. Has not the Lord gone ahead of you?" So Barak went down Mount Tabor, with ten thousand men following him. 15 At Barak's advance, the Lord routed Sisera and all his chariots and army by the sword, and Sisera got down from his chariot and fled on foot. 16 Barak pursued the chariots and army as far as Harosheth Haggoyim, and all Sisera's troops fell by the sword; not a man was left.

Supporting Scripture: Judges 5:6–7, 12, 31

Additional Scripture: Isaiah 6:8; James 1:22–25; Hebrews 11:32–34

Big Idea: Full speed faith refuses to sit at God's green lights – it moves in obedient action so your "YES" becomes the breakthrough that frees whole villages, not just you.

The Deep Dive: When the Light Turns Green

I don't know when you're reading this. Maybe you grabbed this devotional in a storm season, or maybe you picked it up in a quiet moment between meetings, carpools, and text messages. But if you're here, I'm going to say this plainly: You are in a fight for your future, and for the future of your family. And sometimes, winning that fight requires you to move at **full speed**.

When I was a little girl, riding in the car with my dad, he used to get so frustrated with people who wouldn't go when the light turned green. Now, my daddy is a college English professor with a sharp wit, so his commentary was memorable. He'd throw his hands up and say: "What shade of green are you waiting for? It's green. **GO!**" I still laugh thinking about it, because spiritually, so many of us are sitting at green lights. God has already turned on the light:

- You've prayed about it.
- You've fasted about it.
- The pastor preached about your whole situation on Sunday.

✦ Your cousin, your aunt, and your brother told you about someone doing the same thing, and you **knew** that was confirmation you could do it in *your* lane.

And yet, you're frozen at the intersection. Fear on the gas. Overthinking on the brakes. Windows up, hazards blinking, and heaven's like: "Daughter...it's GREEN. GO!" That's what **Full Speed Faith** is about. Not reckless movement. *Responsive* movement. Moving when God says move.

The Judge Who Didn't Flinch

Enter Deborah. Deborah is one of my favorite Bible aunties. She operated at full speed without losing her mind, her femininity, or her prophetic edge. She was a:

Judge – the one people came to for decisions and justice.

Prophet – the one who carried the word of the Lord.

Leader – the one who helped mobilize an entire nation.

Think of her as the wisest judge you know, with a prayer life that could pierce heaven and a battle strategy that could shut down armies. She held court under the Palm of Deborah between Ramah and Bethel. People traveled from all over to hear her rulings.

Back then, when the prophet came to town, and you were living right, you wanted to be seen. You wanted that person to call you out and speak destiny over you. But if you weren't living right? *Whew.* You were ducking behind ushers, hoping the prophet didn't "read your mail" in front of everybody. Deborah carried *both* roles – judge and prophet – and yet she didn't flinch in the face of what her people were living through.

When Village Life Ceased

Israel had sinned, and God allowed them to fall into the hands of King Jabin. His commander, Sisera, had 900 iron chariots – high-tech killing machines for their day – and he ruthlessly oppressed Israel for twenty years. Judges 5:6-7, NIV paints the picture: "In the days of Shamgar son of Anath, in the days of Jael, the highways were abandoned; travelers took to winding paths. Villagers in Israel would not fight; they held back until I, Deborah, arose, until I arose, a mother in Israel." Village life had **ceased**.

Imagine not even being able to live a normal life:

+ No traveling safely on main roads
+ Commerce disrupted
+ Community gatherings ended
+ Fear dictating every decision

I think about modern war zones – like Ukraine – where ordinary people's lives are shattered overnight by political decisions they didn't make. Families packing what they can, running for safety, trying to answer emails and work contracts in the middle of bomb sirens (SAGE Journals). That was Deborah's context. Her people lived under constant threat, exhausted and terrified. No one was stepping up until Deborah **arose**.

The Moses of Her People

Deborah's leadership reminds me of Harriet Tubman – another woman with Full Speed Faith. Harriet escaped slavery in 1849, crossing from Maryland into Pennsylvania. She later described that moment when she crossed the line into freedom: "there was such a glory over everything" (SAGE Journals).

She could have stayed there – free, safe, quiet. But over the next decade, she made trip after dangerous trip back into slave territory, personally leading around 70 people to freedom – family, friends, and strangers who became family on the way north. She was called "Moses" because she refused to make freedom a private thing.

Her famous statement? "I never ran my train off the track, and I never lost a passenger." That's **Full Speed Faith**: not careless movement, but *courageous, obedient* movement. Like Harriet, Deborah understood: Some people's safety is tied to your **"yes."**

The Commander Who Said "I'll Go...If You Go"

God gives Deborah a word for Barak, Israel's military commander:

+ Gather ten thousand men.
+ Go to Mount Tabor.
+ God will deliver Sisera into your hands.

She delivers the word clearly: no fluff, no extras, just what God said.

Barak's response? "If you go with me, I will go; but if you don't go with me, I won't go." *Sir.* This is where we need to say something gently but firmly: **Delayed obedience is still disobedience**. Barak believed the word – but he hesitated to move **without** Deborah's physical presence. Deborah didn't shame him, but she did tell him the truth: *"Certainly I will go with you. But because of the course you are taking, the honor will not be yours, for the Lord will deliver Sisera into the hands of a woman"* (Judges 4:9, NIV).

Sometimes, you're **the one** who's called to step up. Sometimes, you're called to step up **with** someone. Sometimes, you're Deborah; sometimes, you're Barak. Either way, Full Speed Faith recognizes when God is saying, "This is your green light. **Move**."

When Heaven Fights with You

When Deborah finally says, "Up! For this is the day the Lord has given Sisera into your hands. Has not the Lord gone out before you?" (Judges 4:14, NIV), Barak and his men charge. Judges 5 tells us that:

+ The **stars** fought from their courses against Sisera.
+ God sent a storm that turned the River Kishon into a flood.
+ Those 900 iron chariots – Sisera's greatest flex – got stuck.

The very thing the enemy trusted (chariots) became his biggest liability. When Deborah moved at full speed *in obedience*, heaven moved with her. Full Speed Faith Principle: **When you move on God's word, you are never moving alone.**

Godly Submission & Sacred Alignment

Now, let's talk about something we often get twisted: **submission**. We meet Deborah as a national leader, but Scripture also quietly notes she is "the wife of Lappidoth" (Judges 4:4, NIV). She is fully walking in her public calling, yet still rooted in covenant relationships and community.

Submission has been weaponized in a lot of spaces – especially against women. So let's redeem the word a bit. Biblically, *godly* submission is:

+ ***Voluntary alignment*** under God's order and wisdom.
+ ***A posture of humility*** that says, "I don't have to be the only voice in the room."
+ ***Mutual honor*** in healthy relationships, not blind obedience to abuse.

It shows up in different ways:

+ As a wife, honoring her husband in a healthy, non-abusive marriage.
+ As an employee, respecting a boss while still honoring God above company culture.
+ As a ministry leader, submitting to pastors, mentors, and spiritual covering.
+ As a CEO, submitting to the Holy Spirit and wise counsel so that success doesn't shipwreck her soul.

And Deborah models all of these examples beautifully:

+ She hears from God.
+ She speaks with authority.
+ She leads in war.
+ She does so under God's voice, not her ego.

Godly submission is not about shrinking. It's about being **anchored**. It's knowing: I can lead the meeting *and* listen. I can make the call *and* receive counsel. I can carry authority *and* stay under authority.

For single, divorced, widowed, or never-married women, this still applies. Your submission is first and foremost to God:

+ Submitting your decisions to His wisdom

+ Submitting your schedule to His rest
+ Submitting your gifts to His timing

That posture keeps your full speed from turning into full chaos.

Sacred Femininity in a World That Demands You Be "Strong"

Now we need to talk about **femininity**. Biblically, men and women are both made in the image of God (Genesis 1:27). Femininity is not weakness; it's a reflection of God's nurturing, creative, life-bearing, relational heart. But many of us – *especially* Black, Indigenous, Latina, Asian, and other women of color – have been taught, explicitly and implicitly, that we are only valuable when we are **strong**.

The "Strong Black Woman" stereotype says we are supposed to carry everything, endure anything, never break, and certainly never show vulnerability. Research shows this stereotype leads to emotional burnout, health consequences, and constant pressure to "hold it all together" for everyone else.

For Indigenous women, colonialism and forced displacement have often stripped them of land, community, and traditional roles, while imposing patriarchal systems that devalued their voices and labor.

For many Mexican and Latina women, cultural expectations like *marianismo* frame them as self-sacrificing caregivers, responsible for everyone's well-being – often at great personal cost.

For South Asian women and other immigrant women of color, migration stories often involve leaving everything familiar behind, working multiple jobs, and carrying the emotional and economic weight of extended family across borders.

Intersectional research confirms what we live: women of color often face overlapping racism and sexism that pressure us to be perpetually resilient, available, and "on."

So, we show up:

+ As pillars of strength in our families.
+ As shock absorbers in our communities.
+ As free therapists in our churches and workplaces.

Many of us have been "strong" because we felt we had **no other choice**. But here is the invitation of kingdom femininity: You are allowed to be strong **and** soft. You are allowed to lead **and** be held. You are allowed to fight **and** rest. To embrace your femininity – your God-given beauty, softness, intuition, creativity, and capacity for joy – is not a luxury. It's part of your **birthright** as a daughter of God.

You may still be the caretaker, decision-maker, boss, visionary, homemaker, leader, wife, working mom, coach, elder, or "go-to" person. But even in that, God is whispering *Daughter, you are valuable in My sight. In My presence, you are not a machine that produces miracles for everyone else. Here, you can* **rest**.

Don't Lose Your Femininity in the Fight

So, let's say this plainly: We cannot afford to lose our femininity while we're fighting the battles of life. Many of us have been in fight mode for so long that we only know how to show up armored. Our tone, our posture, our energy – always braced, always ready to respond, always on alert.

A woman living in a permanent state of fight is a woman who is not resting. And a woman who is not resting has a hard time receiving love – including from herself.

That's not a rebuke. That's a **rescue mission**. You deserve to be loved. You deserve to be cared for. You deserve to be more than "the strong one."

If I were doing a self-love altar call right now, I'd invite all my overachieving, over functioning, overperforming, micro-managing, "I got it, I'll do it myself" sisters to come to the front. Full Speed Faith is not about you doing the **most**. It's about you doing what **God** said – at the pace He said – with the grace He gives. Sometimes, that means relinquishing control. Sometimes, that means slowing down to heal. Sometimes, that means saying, "I matter too." You cannot answer a Full Speed Faith moment if you're too exhausted to move when God says GO.

Kingdom Strategies for Full Speed Faith

1. **Speak Up Boldly.** Deborah didn't whisper God's Word – she *declared* it. When God gives you a Word for your life, your family, your work, or someone you're called to encourage, **speak it**:
   - » Don't water it down so it's more comfortable.
   - » Don't add extra spice God didn't give you.
   - » Deliver the word with humility and confidence – and let God back it up.

2. **Show Up Even When It's Not "Your" Assignment.** When Barak said, "I'll only go if you go," Deborah could have said, "Not my circus, not my problem." Instead, she went. Sometimes, you're the one God uses to carry the vision. Sometimes, you're the one called to be the assist – the base in cheer, the one holding others steady so they can stand tall. Be willing to:
   - » Lead when He says lead.
   - » Support when He says support.
   - » Share the victory when He says, "This one is a team win."

3. **Move When God Says Move.** Deborah discerned the God-moment and called for action: "Up! For this is the day…" She didn't wait for better weather, more perfect conditions, or unanimous approval ratings. When your green light comes:

» Stop asking what shade of green it is.

» Stop waiting for every single person to agree.

» GO – with wisdom, submission to God, and care for your own humanity.

Full Speed Faith Takeaways

1. **Your freedom isn't just for you.**
Deborah and Harriet both refused to make their freedom private. Your breakthrough is meant to create space, strategy, and safety for others.

2. **You can be a leader and walk in godly submission.**
Deborah proves greatness and submission aren't enemies. You can be powerful, prophetic, and strategic – and still be anchored under God, wise counsel, and healthy partnership.

3. **Heaven moves when you move on God's word.**
When Deborah commanded, God sent storms and stars into the battle. Your full speed "yes" activates resources you cannot see yet.

Full Speed Faith Prayer

Lord,

I confess that I have sat at too many green lights. You have confirmed, nudged, whispered, and shouted – and still, fear and fatigue have kept me stuck at the intersection of promise and purpose. Today, I am activating Full Speed Faith. Like Deborah, give me:

- *The courage to speak what You say.*
- *The humility to submit to Your order and godly leadership.*
- *The discernment to know when to lead and when to support.*
- *The wisdom to care for my own body, mind, and soul along the way.*

I renounce the lie that I must always be the "strong one." I receive Your invitation to be both strong and soft, powerful and tender, called and cared for. Teach me godly submission – to You first, and to the healthy leaders, partners, and communities You place in my life. Help me lay down survival patterns that keep me in constant fight mode. I declare: I am not asking what shade of green. When You say GO, I will move. Up – for this is the day You have given me victory.

In Jesus' name, Amen.

Full Speed Faith: Journal

Identify Your Green Lights and Journal:
- What has God already confirmed that you're still sitting on?
- What are you afraid will happen if you actually go full speed?
- Write down **one** assignment you already know is a green light.

Discern Your Submissions and Journal:
- Where is God asking you to practice healthy submission – to His voice, to wise counsel, to a process, to rest?
- Where have you confused people-pleasing or control with faithfulness?
- Write a sentence that starts: *Lord, I choose to submit _______________ to You in this season.*

Reclaim Your Femininity and Journal:
- Where have you been living in constant fight mode?
- In what ways has the "strong woman" expectation cost you rest, joy, softness, or health?
- Ask God: *What does being "fully woman" look like for me – here, now, in this life?*
- Write one small act of self-care or softness you will practice this week (rest, beauty, creativity, pleasure, time in the Word with no agenda).

Full Speed Faith Challenge & Activation

1. **Name Your Green Light** – Choose one confirmed assignment and write it somewhere visible.
2. **Take One "GO" Step** – Before the week ends, take one concrete step toward it: send the email, schedule the meeting, apply for the thing, create the outline.
3. **Ask for Help** – Identify one area where you've been trying to be the "strong one" and ask for support – from God, a therapist, a trusted friend, or a mentor.
4. **Schedule Your Softness** – Put one act of rest or joy on your calendar and protect it like a meeting with God.

> **Remember:** You cannot answer a Full Speed Faith moment if you are too depleted to move.

God is not asking you to be a machine. He is inviting you to be a **whole woman** – submitted, steady, rested, and ready – when He says GO.

Tomorrow's Teaser:
Ferocious Faith with Jael

Remember when Deborah told Barak that because of his hesitation, the glory would go to a woman? Tomorrow, we will meet **her**. Jael was a tent-dwelling wife with a hammer and a tent peg – ordinary tools in ordinary hands that God used for extraordinary deliverance. So, get ready for **Day 7: Ferocious Faith!** Sometimes, a breakthrough doesn't come from the battlefield; it comes from a woman in her everyday space, moving in bold, obedient power. Your tent-peg moment is coming.

DAY 7

FEROCIOUS FAITH

Sometimes, Something Has to Die for Your Future to Live

Ferocious (fuh-ROH-shuhs) – *adjective*
- Savagely fierce, cruel, or violent
- Extremely intense or powerful
- Marked by unrelenting intensity or determination
- Exhibiting or given to extreme fierceness

Kingdom Definition: Faith that refuses to play nice with the enemy of your destiny – strategic, strong, and decisive enough to use what's in your hand to secure forty years of peace for your entire generation.

Ferocious Faith Scripture Foundation: (Primary) Judges 5:24–27, 31 (NIV)

24 Most blessed of women be Jael, the wife of Heber the Kenite, most blessed of tent-dwelling women. 25 He asked for water, and she gave him milk; in a bowl fit for nobles she brought him curdled milk. 26 Her hand reached for the tent peg, her right hand for the workman's hammer. She struck Sisera, she crushed his head, she shattered and pierced his temple. 27 At her feet he sank, he fell; there he lay. At her feet he sank, he fell; where he sank, there he fell – dead.

31 "So may all your enemies perish, Lord! But may all who love you be like the sun when it rises in its strength." Then the land had peace forty years.

Supporting Scripture: Judges 4:17–22

Additional Scripture: Matthew 11:12; Ephesians 6:12; 1 Peter 5:8

> **Big Idea:** Ferocious faith doesn't negotiate with what threatens your destiny – it uses wisdom, strength, and what's already in your hand to cut off the enemy's access and secure peace for generations.

A Gentle Note Before We Begin

Family, today's story is intense. We're talking about a woman who takes a tent peg and ends a man's life. For survivors of violence, this can stir up emotions and memories. I want you to know:

+ We are **not** glorifying violence.
+ We are **not** celebrating harm to people.
+ We *are* looking at this story through the lens of **spiritual warfare** and courageous, decisive action against what threatens your God-given future.

If at any point your heart feels overwhelmed, pause. *Breathe.* Come back later, or invite a trusted friend, therapist, or prayer partner into this space with you. You are not weak for protecting your heart.

The Deep Dive: The Woman with the Tent Peg

I remember when I first heard the story of Jael and thought, "Oh my God – she's a *bad* somebody." Everything in you wants to say, "There's no way I could hurt somebody, no way I could take someone's life." And in everyday life, that is a good and right instinct. Most of us don't wake up looking for a fight.

But let me invite you into a different angle. If you are a mother and there is an intruder in your home, you don't know their intentions. All you know is that:

+ They are not supposed to be there.
+ They entered without permission.
+ They pose a threat to the people you love.

In that moment, you may quickly decide that you are prepared to **eliminate the threat**. They had access to any house, but **they picked the wrong house**. Because you will fearlessly and ferociously protect what is yours.

Trained for the "Last Resort"

Now, depending on your wiring, you might be the one who hides behind the door and calls 911. OR you might be the one who runs toward the danger. Some folks are just built to **run to the fire** – toward the car accident and the gunshots – trying to help, stop, rescue, or pull somebody out. I'm married to one of those people.

My husband is the "runs to the scene" type. He has also made sure I am trained – properly and safely – to protect myself with firearms and self-defense. Not because I'm out here looking for a fight, but because he never wants me, our kids, our grandkids, or our parents to be defenseless.

He told me plainly: "If somebody ever gets the jump on me, or if there's more than one attacker, I need to know you can step in if you have to. I'm the first line of defense – but I don't ever want you or our family to be helpless if I'm not there." Let me be clear:

+ Returning violence is the **very last resort**.
+ The gun range still gives me anxiety – my whole body feels that sound.
+ I do *not* desire to use a firearm on anyone.

However, I've gotten comfortable with the training because I understand: As a mother, wife, daughter, and caretaker, I may face a moment where I must protect myself and the people entrusted to me – with every resource and skill the Lord provides.

Jael is *that* kind of woman. She's not bloodthirsty. She's not looking for a fight. But when the fight **runs into her tent**, she is not caught unprepared.

When the Enemy Runs to the Wrong House

Jael's story is connected to Deborah's. Sisera, the commander of King Jabin's army, has been terrorizing Israel with 900 iron chariots. When God sends rain and the battlefield turns to mud, those chariots – his big flex – get stuck. His army is being routed. What does Sisera do? He runs. He abandons his troops on the field. Leaves his men to die while he tries to save himself. That's not just wicked – that's cowardly leadership.

Running for his life, he stumbles upon the tent of Jael, the wife of Heber the Kenite. There is supposed to be peace between his king and her household, so he thinks he's found a safe house. He is exhausted. Desperate. Disarmed. And he sees a woman who – on the surface – looks harmless. Soft. Non-threatening. This feels a little like the Delilah story in reverse:

+ In Delilah's story, a woman's intimacy is weaponized *against* God's man.
+ In Jael's story, a woman's courage is weaponized *for* God's people.

Jael reminds every man reading this – and every mother raising sons: You can't just lay your head **anywhere**. Not every soft place is a safe place.

Strategy Over Strength

Sisera asks Jael for water. She gives him milk in a bowl fit for a noble – comforting, soothing, probably warm and rich. She covers him with a blankct. She makes him feel safe enough to sleep. At first glance, that looks like simple hospitality. But look closer. Jael is not just being nice. She is being **strategic**. We often think strategy looks loud:

+ Yelling
+ Clapping back
+ Exposing people on social media
+ Going toe-to-toe with trolls and toxic folks

But Jael shows us another side: Sometimes, ferocious faith is **quiet**. Sometimes, it looks like calm, composed, deliberate positioning. Why? Because she's dealing with:

+ A dangerous enemy
+ Someone physically stronger than she is
+ Someone backed by a history of violence and oppression

She cannot out-muscle him. So she out-maneuvers him. She uses her:

+ **Softness** to lower his guard
+ **Hospitality** to calm his nerves

✦ **Femininity** and everyday skills to set the stage

This is not manipulation for selfish gain. This is wartime wisdom. This is a battle strategy in a tent.

Sometimes, as women, we get in trouble trying to fight as men do – volume for volume, aggression for aggression, ego for ego. That's not always our lane. God has given us:

✦ Intuition
✦ Emotional intelligence
✦ Discernment
✦ Ability to read a room, read a tone, and read a spirit

Ferocious faith says: "I don't just have *feelings* – I have **strategy**." I'm not yelling just to yell. I'm not swinging just to swing. I'm listening to God's instruction on *when*, *where*, and *how* to move. Jael shows us:

✦ Strength without strategy can get you hurt.
✦ Strategy harnessed to courage can set a nation free.

The Tent Peg Moment

Here's where the story gets graphic. Sisera falls into a deep sleep in Jael's tent. She quietly reaches for what she knows – a **tent peg** and a **hammer** – and in one fierce, decisive act, she drives the peg through his temple and into the ground. One blow. One moment. One brutal, final decision. I want you to sit with a few things here.

1. **This was not random violence.** This was war. Sisera represented years of oppression, slaughter, and terror for her people. As long as he lived, the threat remained.
2. **This was deeply personal and deeply communal.** Her tent, her land, her people. She didn't go looking for him – he brought his threat into her space.
3. **This was physically demanding.** Driving a peg through a skull into the ground took serious strength, stability, and courage.

Spiritually, this is what a **tent peg moment** looks like: You finally decide, "*This thing cannot survive in my life one more day.*" It might be:

+ A toxic relationship that keeps cycling back.
+ A secret sin you've been managing instead of crucifying.
+ A mindset that tells you you're unworthy, unlovable, or always "too much."
+ A family pattern (addiction, financial chaos, rage, codependency) that has terrorized generations.

You've tried:
+ Negotiating with it
+ Reasoning with it
+ Making room for it
+ Praying about it but never taking action

A tent peg moment is when you say, "No more. Not in my tent. Not in my generation. This dies **here**."

And listen – tent peg moments are usually:

+ Messy
+ Emotional
+ Not Instagram-cute
+ Often misunderstood by folks who benefitted from your silence

But they are holy. Why? Because some things cannot be:

+ Coached out
+ Cuddled out
+ Coped with

They must be **killed** – spiritually, emotionally, relationally. You may not ever drive a physical peg through anyone's skull (please don't), but in the Spirit, you are absolutely called to put a peg through:

+ The enemy's access
+ Old agreements
+ Old idols

Jael's tent peg moment is an invitation for you to have one too.

Getting Strong for Your Ferocious Faith

Jael's act reminds us: **spiritual assignments often demand physical capacity.** I realized I could not live out my assignment feeling weak, inflamed, and exhausted. Perimenopause was kicking my butt. I was inconsistent with:

+ The gym
+ Supplements
+ Sleep
+ Food choices

Traveling a lot meant long drives, quick food, and "I'll fix it later" choices. The scale was climbing. Hot flashes were disrespectful. Joints were popping. Energy was dipping.

Then my husband – the trainer that he is – broke something down that changed my thinking. He said: "You don't inherit disease – you inherit **lifestyle**. You inherit the behaviors, patterns, and eating habits that create an environment for those diseases."

My maternal grandmother had diabetes. My mother doesn't – because her lifestyle is different. On my dad's side, we can see similarities between health patterns and habits. My husband said, "If I don't want what runs in my family, I have to live differently from my family."

So I got serious. I started a wellness journey and didn't look back. Pounds dropped. Hot flashes calmed. Clarity returned.

Why am I telling you this in Jael's chapter? Because: You cannot swing a tent peg if you're too weak to lift your hand. Your ferocious faith needs a body that can carry it. Especially if you're 40 and over, perimenopause and menopause are coming whether we RSVP or not. You've got to get strong:

+ Physically
+ Mentally
+ Emotionally
+ Spiritually

Use What You Have

Notice what Jael **didn't** do:
+ She didn't run out to find a soldier's sword.
+ She didn't go hunt down a fancy new weapon.
+ She didn't say, "I'll move when I get better tools."

She grabbed a **tent peg** and a **hammer** – tools she used every day. She used what she had, where she was, with what she knew. This is Ferocious Faith:
+ You stop waiting for "someday."
+ You stop despising your ordinary tools.
+ You recognize your tent peg: your voice, your degree, your lived experience, your compassion, your spreadsheets, your classroom, your salon chair, your kitchen table, your podcast, your prayer life.

Jael didn't know she'd be chosen for this task. But when the moment presented itself, she rose to the occasion. Strong enough. Brave enough. Strategic enough. And so are you.

The Song of Victory

Judges 5:24–27, 31 NIV says:
> *"Most blessed of women be Jael,*
> *the wife of Heber the Kenite,*
> *most blessed of tent-dwelling women.*
> *He asked for water, and she gave him milk;*
> *in a bowl fit for nobles she brought him curdled milk.*

Her hand reached for the tent peg,
her right hand for the workman's hammer.
She struck Sisera, she crushed his head,
she shattered and pierced his temple.
At her feet he sank, he fell; there he lay.
At her feet he sank, he fell;
where he sank, there he fell – dead."
"So may all your enemies perish, Lord!
But may all who love you be like the sun when it
rises in its strength."
Then the land had peace for forty years."

God didn't just tolerate what she did. He **honored** it in a victory song.

Forty Years of Peace

One woman's decisive, ferocious act of faith set off a chain reaction that gave the land **forty years of peace**. *Forty.* That's a whole generation growing up never knowing the terror their parents endured. Imagine if she had hesitated. Imagine if she had said, "This is too messy, too violent, too much responsibility for me." Family, hear this in love: Sometimes, your future, and the future of your whole community, hinges on you refusing to keep making room for what God has already marked for death.

You might be "just one woman" praying in your kitchen, setting boundaries, going to therapy, leaving toxic spaces, getting your health together, paying off debt, starting a business, writing a book, and/or telling the truth. All while heaven might be singing over you, *Most blessed of women be ____________, who drove a peg through what was killing her people!*

Kingdom Strategies for Ferocious Faith

1. **Have a Strategy.** Jael didn't wing it. She didn't flail. She moved with intention. Sometimes, ferocious faith looks soft on the outside and surgical on the inside. Ask yourself: What's my **battle plan** for this issue? Have I asked God for a strategy – or just vented? Am I using my intuition, wisdom, and resources – or just reacting?

2. **Move Fast and Don't Hesitate.** Once the moment came, she didn't delay. When it's time to drive a tent peg through something that's been oppressing you or your family, don't overthink it. Don't give fear time to talk you out of it. Don't keep tucking it under a blanket and calling it "grace." Grace is not an agreement. Grace gives you power to act – not excuses to avoid.

3. **Use What You Have and Be Strong Enough to Use It.** She didn't have a sword. She had household tools. And she was strong enough to swing them. Stop waiting for "better equipment" before you obey. Use the tools you already know. Start with the strength you already have. Commit to growing stronger so you can carry what God is placing on you.

Ferocious Faith Takeaways

1. **Your ferocious faith can secure peace for generations.** One decisive act gave her people forty years of peace. The stand you take now can change the story for your children and your children's children.

2. **You don't inherit disease – you inherit lifestyle.** The patterns that plague your family aren't just in your DNA; they're in your habits. Change the lifestyle, change the outcome. Be the one who flips the script.

3. **Sometimes, something has to die for your future to live.** As long as Sisera was breathing, the threat remained. Some mindsets, relationships, agreements, and patterns cannot be negotiated with. They must be crucified.

Ferocious Faith Prayer

Lord,

*I thank You for 7 days of faith activation. I started with a foundation that needed building, moved through fractures that needed fixing, and now I stand ready for my future with **ferocious faith**. Like Jael, give me **strategy** when I need wisdom and **strength** when I need to strike. Help me use what's already in my hand – my gifts, my resources, my position – to close the door on the enemies of my destiny.*

I will not play nice with what threatens my purpose, my family, or my future. I decree that every "Sisera" that has run into my territory thinking it was a safe place to rest – every generational curse, every limiting belief, every toxic pattern, every assignment of the enemy – TODAY receives a tent peg. I am done negotiating. I am done tolerating. I am done being passive. I declare forty years of peace over my household. I declare that my children and my children's children will walk in the freedom I am securing by faith today. May all who love You be like the sun when it rises in its strength. My faith is ACTIVATED. My faith is FEROCIOUS. And it stops with ME.

In Jesus' name, Amen.

Ferocious Faith Reflection & Activation

Family, look at **you**. You have made it through **seven whole days of Future Forward Faith**. Over this week, you have:

+ Faced some hard truths about your story and your future.
+ Dared to believe that God has more for you than survival.
+ Chosen to stand up, speak up, and move differently.

You may have started this journey barely breathing – codependent, coexisting, drowning in someone else's rejection, worn out from caring for everybody but yourself.

But now? You understand that your prayers, your choices, and your life require a **violent stand** against the darkness trying to eclipse your future. When – not if – your faith is tested after this, the goal is not perfection, it's **posture**:

+ That you stood.
+ That you swung your tent peg.
+ That you refused to partner with what was killing you.

You are producing a future that would not exist without your "yes" – and your willingness to say **"no more"** to the things that have had you bound.

Ferocious Faith: Journal

+ What has been "sleeping in your tent" – what threat have you been tolerating that needs to be eliminated?
+ What's already in your hand that you haven't recognized as a weapon or a tool?
+ What generational pattern or lifestyle are you committed to ending with you?
+ What area of your life needs you to get physically, mentally, or spiritually stronger?

Ferocious Faith Final Challenge

Your final challenge is to **activate** your ferocious faith:

1. **Write Your Declaration of War** – Name the "Sisera" in your life – the thing that has oppressed you or your family – and declare its end **TODAY**.

2. **Take One Tent Peg Action** – Before this week is over, do the decisive thing you've been avoiding:

   » Have that hard conversation.
   » Make the difficult decision.
   » End the toxic tie.
   » Schedule the therapy.
   » Clean out the environment that keeps you stuck.

3. **Start Your Strength Journey**. Commit to getting stronger:

   » Walk
   » Stretch
   » Join a gym or class
   » Clean up your eating
   » Go to bed on time

   Jael couldn't have done what she did if she were weak. Neither can you.

4. **Break One Generational Pattern**. Identify one inherited lifestyle habit that's been passed down in your family and be the one who stops it.

5. **Pray Violent Prayers**. Not violent against people – but violent against the **spiritual enemies** of your destiny. Take a ferocious stand in your prayer life this week.

Your Ferocious Faith Declaration

I, ____,

declare on this day that my faith is fully activated.

I have built my foundation.

I have fixed my fractures.

I am ready for my future.

I will be ferocious about my purpose, my family,

and myself.

NOT ME. NOT MY FAMILY. NOT THIS GENERATION.

It stops with ME.

Signed: ____

Date: ____

"So may all your enemies perish, Lord!
But may all who love you be like the sun when
it rises in its strength."

— JUDGES 5:31

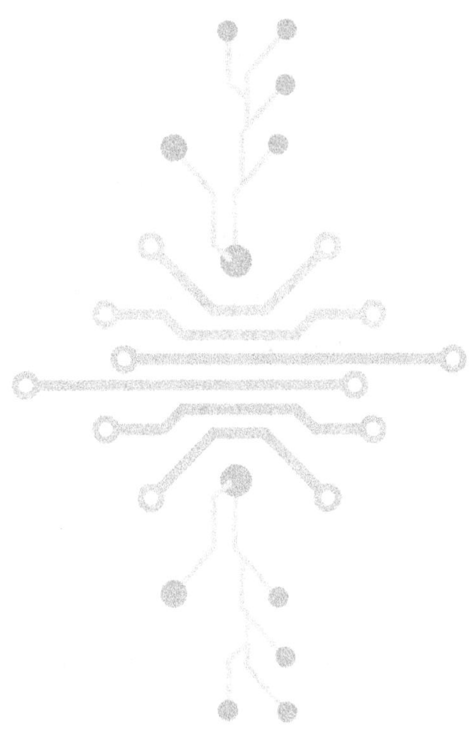

FUTURE-PROOF FAITH

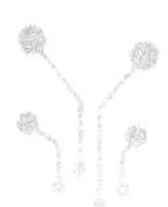

Before you close this book, don't miss the bonus mini-day: **Futureproof Faith**. We're going to look at the Roman centurion whose faith made Jesus marvel. He shows us what it means to:

- Stand under authority
- Speak the word
- Secure outcomes without Jesus even stepping into the house

If Jael shows us how to strike a decisive blow in the heat of battle, the centurion shows us how to build a faith that not only fights for **today** but **future-proofs** your family, your purpose, and your legacy. Your ferocious faith has been activated. Now, let's learn how to make it **last**.

A Final Invitation

Instead of a traditional conclusion – the kind you'd usually find at the end of a devotional – I felt led to do something different for **Future Forward Faith**. Right around the middle of writing this week, I kept hearing one word in my spirit: **"Futureproof."**

I sat with it for a few days, prayed into it, and realized this wasn't just a catchy phrase. It was an instruction. This week couldn't end with a simple "The End." It needed a faith **sealant** – something that would help you protect, guard, and carry what God has started in you into whatever comes next.

So here's my invitation: If you are full – and you truly can't take in one more thing – you are absolutely free to close this devotional right here. You've completed **seven days of Future Forward Faith**, and that is no small thing. You showed up. You read. You wrestled. You reflected. You let God talk to you about your future.

But, if you've got just a little room left; If your spirit is saying, "I don't want to lose this momentum;" If you're craving one more round of activation – like dessert after a really good meal – I'd love for you to close out this journey with me in a special **bonus devotional: "Futureproof Faith."** Think of it as your spiritual after-care and your faith insurance policy – a way to take everything God has stirred this week and anchor it in a faith that can stand storms, delays, transitions, and whatever the next season holds. If you're ready, turn the page. Let's futureproof what God just started in you.

FUTURE-PROOF FAITH

The Expectation of Good

Future-Proof (FYOO-chur-proof) – *adjective/verb*
+ Built to last — designed to hold up no matter what changes come
+ Getting ahead of what's coming so you're not knocked off your feet when it arrives
+ Making something flexible and strong enough to handle whatever shows up next

Kingdom Definition: A faith so anchored in the Word, authority, and goodness of God that no storm, shift, or season can render it obsolete – the kind of believing that doesn't just survive the future but is already built for it.

Future-Proof Faith Scripture Lesson: Matthew 8:5–13, ESV

5 When he had entered Capernaum, a centurion came forward to him, appealing to him, 6 "Lord, my servant is lying paralyzed at home, suffering terribly." 7 And he said to him, "I will come and heal him." 8 But the centurion replied, "Lord, I am not worthy to have you come under my roof, but only say the word, and my servant will be healed. 9 For I too am a man under authority, with soldiers under me. And I say to one, 'Go,' and he goes, and to another, 'Come,' and he comes, and to my servant, 'Do this,' and he does it." 10 When Jesus heard this, he marveled and said to those who followed him, "Truly, I tell you, with no one in Israel have I found such faith. 11 I tell you, many will come from east and west and recline at table with Abraham, Isaac, and Jacob in the kingdom of heaven, 12 while the sons of the kingdom will be thrown into the outer darkness. In that place there will be weeping and gnashing of teeth." 13 And to the centurion Jesus said, "Go; let it be done for you as you have believed." And the servant was healed at that very moment.

Supporting Scripture: James 1:2–4
Additional Scripture: Matthew 7:24–25

We made it, sis. We made it to the end of this journey – and I pray you feel lighter. More hopeful. More anchored. Full of expectation for what God is about to do. But before you close this book, I need to hand you one more thing. Consider this your send-off, your commissioning, your tank full of gas for wherever God is taking you next.

The Faith That Made Jesus Marvel

In Matthew 8:5–13, a Roman centurion approaches Jesus. His servant is sick, paralyzed, and suffering terribly. This centurion isn't a nobody. He's a man of rank, authority, and power. He commands at least a hundred soldiers. When he speaks, people move.

But watch what happens when he meets Jesus: "Lord, I am not worthy to have You come under my roof, but only say the word, and my servant will be healed. For I also am a man under authority, having soldiers under me. And I say to this one, 'Go,' and he goes, and to another, 'Come,' and he comes…"

And Jesus? The Bible says **He marveled**. The Son of God – who has seen everything from the foundation of the world – was amazed at this man's faith. He turned to the crowd and said, "I tell you, I have not found such great faith, no, not in Israel." That's the kind of faith I want you to walk out of here with. In the Gospels, you see three different measures of faith:

+ **Jairus**, who needs Jesus to come to his house to heal his daughter.
+ **The woman with the issue of blood**, who believes, "If I can just touch the hem of His garment, I'll be made whole."
+ **This centurion**, who believes Jesus doesn't even have to move His feet – He only has to **speak a word**.

Three different expressions. One Jesus. And God meets each of them at their measure of faith. Today, as you close this book, I believe God is inviting you into **futureproof faith** – a faith that expects Him to move, even when all you're holding onto is His **word**.

The R.O.C.K. Recipe for Futureproof Faith

So, what made this centurion's faith so remarkable? Let's pull out the recipe. Here's an easy way to remember it: **R.O.C.K. Faith = Futureproof Faith**

R – Regulate your emotions

His servant was dying. He had every right to panic, spiral, or fall apart. But instead of freaking out, he got **strategic**. He didn't pretend he wasn't hurting – but he didn't let his feelings drive the decision. That's emotional regulation: Feel it. Bring it to God. Then move by **faith**, not by fear.

O – Only go to the Source first

He could've called in doctors, soldiers, money, or political favors. Instead, he bypassed every earthly solution and went straight to **Jesus**. Futureproof faith doesn't make God the last phone call after we've exhausted everything else. It makes Him the **first stop**.

C – Come under His authority

He understood authority because he lived under it and walked in it. That's why he didn't need Jesus to show up physically. He knew that when a person in authority speaks, things move. When you come under Christ's authority – His Word, His will, His way – you stop needing a sign and start trusting His **say-so**.

K – Keep expecting good

There's a Greek word for this: **elpis** – the expectation of good. The centurion didn't come hoping for a shaky "maybe." He came expecting a **yes** from a good God. Futureproof faith keeps expecting God's goodness, even when you don't know how He's going to work it out. So when you think about the kind of faith you're walking in, remember:

> **R.O.C.K. Faith = Futureproof Faith.**

Regulate your emotions. Only go to the Source first. Come under His authority. Keep expecting good. This is the kind of faith that doesn't just get you through today – it **anchors** you for tomorrow.

Build on the Rock

James 1:2–4 tells us to *count it all joy* when trials come – not **IF** they come, but **WHEN** they come. Storms are coming, beloved. That's not a threat; it's reality. Jesus told a parable of two houses – one built on sand and one built on rock. The storm hit **both** houses. The difference wasn't the weather. It was the foundation.

+ Sand washes away when the water rises.
+ Rock stands steady when the wind beats against it.

Right now, you're making a declaration: "I will not build my faith on sand – on feelings, trends, or convenience. I'm building on the **Rock**." R.O.C.K. faith doesn't deny the wave. It anchors to the One who **walks on it**.

This Is Your Time

I didn't write this devotional to get rich. I wrote it because I felt compelled by God to finish what I started. I started this project a long time ago, but I knew it wasn't just a cute idea – it was an **assignment**. And I don't believe you just stumbled into this book, either. You're on assignment too. If I can say anything to you, it's this: **Don't give up.** It is time to get ready for your **next**. God has something great in store for you – and it's not just for you. It's for everyone connected to you.

There are people on the earth **assigned** to you. The only way they get what they need is if you step out on faith, if you activate, if you move. Don't make God pick somebody else – because He will if you absolutely refuse. But He called **you**. He equipped **you**. He predestined **you** before the foundation of the world to do the thing He placed in your heart. He knew that in this particular time, this particular moment, this particular season, there would be people who need you to step up and do what He's calling you to do. You just needed to be **activated**.

A Simple Way to Be a Blessing

If this journey has blessed you, I have one simple request: **Don't let it stop with you.**

+ Buy a copy for someone who needs their faith activated.
+ Or lend your copy – with a boundary and a little humor: "Sis, I'm letting you borrow this for 10 days…but I'm gonna need my book back."

Because this isn't just a cute read, this is a manual. A weapon. A lifeline. You're not just sharing a book; you're starting a **faith chain reaction** – one woman at a time.

Prayer: Futureproof My Faith

Lord,

Thank You for walking with me through this journey. Thank You for every truth, every tear, every moment You've used to build my faith. Today, I ask You to futureproof my faith.
Teach me to respond like that centurion – not ruled by emotion, but running straight to You.
*Help me understand Your authority, rest under it, and move in it. Fill me with **"elpis – the expectation of good"** – even when the storm clouds gather. I choose to build on the Rock. I choose to believe that You have good things planned for me. I choose to say yes to the assignment over my life. Make my faith steady, strong, and unshakeable so that everyone connected to me sees Your goodness through my obedience.*

In Jesus' name, Amen.

Your Declaration & Activation

Write this somewhere you'll see it often – in your journal, on a sticky note, on your mirror:

> **This is my time.**
> **This is my charge.**
> **This is my call.**
> **This is my sign.**
> **I will do it – by faith.**

Now, before the is over, take **one concrete step** toward the thing God has been nudging you to do:

+ Make the call
+ Send the email
+ Enroll in the class
+ Schedule the session
+ Start the draft
+ Have the conversation

Don't wait for the perfect moment. This *is* the moment. Your faith is activated. Your foundation is R.O.C.K. solid. Your future is calling. **Go do it.**

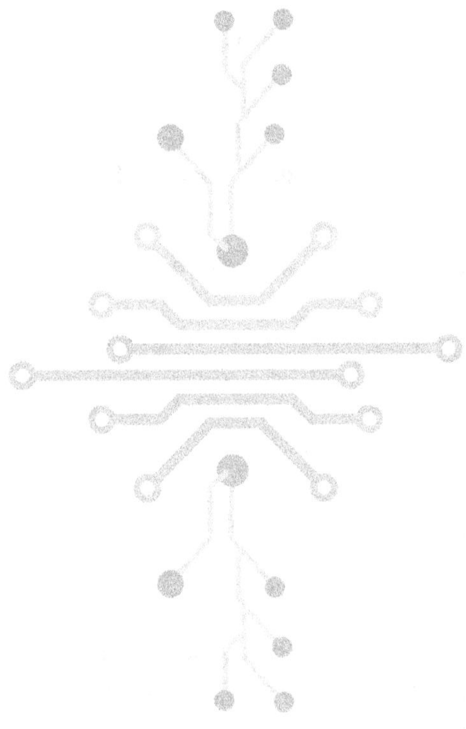

DISCOVER THE FULL ACTIVATE YOUR FAITH SERIES

If you picked up **Future Forward Faith** as a standalone devotional, first of all, I'm so glad you did. This is actually **Devotion 3** in the *Activate Your Faith* journey, which you can experience in two ways:

1. The Full 21-Day Devotional

Activate Your Faith: The Art of Facing Fiery Trials (21-Day Devotional – matchstick + flame cover)

This is the *all-in-one* edition – the complete 21-day experience in a single volume. If you want to walk straight through Faith Foundation, Fragments, and Future Forward Faith without stopping, this is your journal-style companion for the whole journey.

2. The 7-Day Devotionals by Week

You can also work through the series **one focused week at a time**:

- **Devotion I – Faith Foundation: 7 Days of Facing Fears & Overcoming Doubts**. A 7-day reset to rebuild what you believe about God and yourself, so your faith is anchored in who He is – not in fear, shame, or past failures.
- **Devotion II – Fragments: 7 Days of Fixing Fractured Faith**. This isn't another "just pray harder" devotional while you're bleeding out – it's **rescue for kidnapped faith**. Fragments is intensive care for the parts of you that kept moving while your faith was taken hostage: seven days to stop the quiet hemorrhaging, triage the fractures, and let God reset what healed wrong so you can stand whole again.
- **Devotion III – Future Forward Faith: 7 Days to Believe Beyond Now for What's Next**. Future Forward Faith helps you break out of reverse, align with heaven's strategy, and move toward your destiny with a faith that's bold enough to ask, brave enough to act, and steady enough to carry you all the way there.

You can start anywhere – full 21 days or one week at a time. Each resource was crafted to help you get **anchored, healed, and activated** so you can walk in alignment and on assignment.

We pray this book was a blessing to you! If you need multiple copies or would like to book author Rainah Davis as a speaker for your next event, please email:

rainah@rainahdavis.com

or DM her via her Instagram account @RainahMDavis.

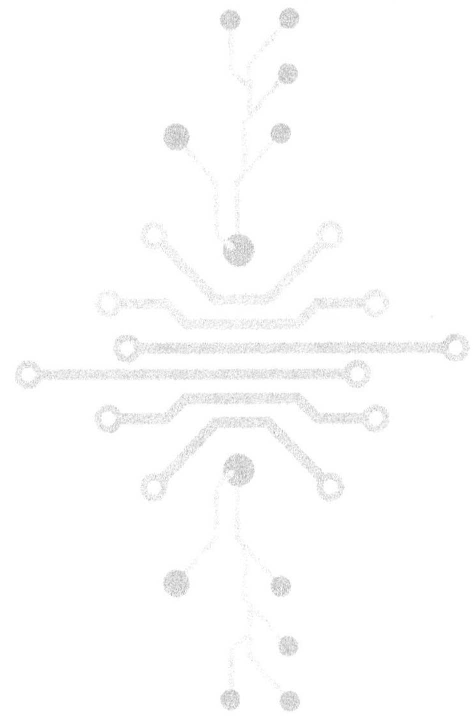

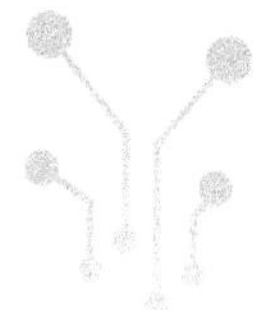

LET'S STAY CONNECTED

I don't just want to be a voice on your bookshelf; I'd love to stay connected as you keep walking this out. You can find me here:

- **Instagram:** @rainahdavis
- **Facebook:** rainahsdavis
- **LinkedIn:** rainahmdavis
- **Website / Stay Connected Hub:** rainahdavis.com

Come say hi, share what God did in your life through this devotional, and keep an eye out for new resources, books, and opportunities to grow in faith, purpose, and whole-life wellness.

We're just getting started.

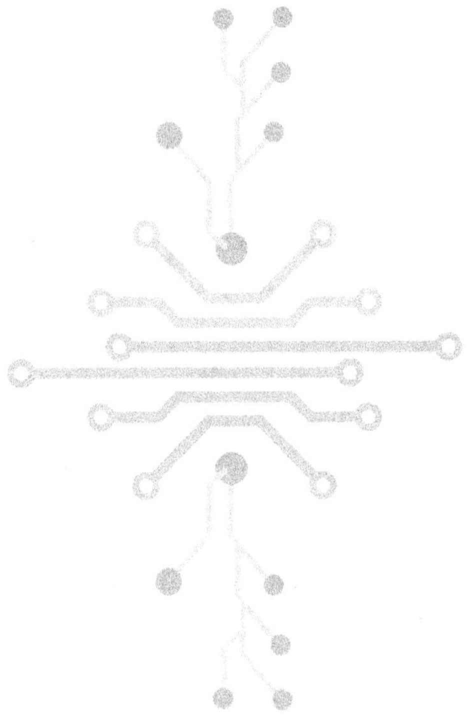

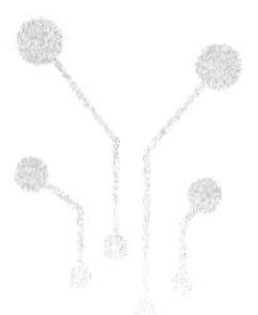

REFERENCE & RESOURCE GUIDE

I believe in doing my homework – and I know many of you do too. The books, articles, and resources listed in this section are here to give you language, context, and deeper study around the themes we touched on in this devotional: faith, femininity, strength, rest, mental health, culture, and generational healing. Some of these sources are academic, some are practical, some are written from a faith lens, and others from a more secular or clinical perspective.

While I don't agree with every idea or conclusion in these works, I found them helpful in shaping my thinking, finding words for our lived experiences, and honoring the stories of women across cultures. My prayer is that as you explore, the Holy Spirit will highlight what aligns with Scripture and your assignment, and release what does not. Use this guide as a springboard for your own study, conversations with your sisters, and ongoing healing – not as a replacement for God's voice, but as one more tool to help you live free, whole, and on purpose.

Harriet Tubman, Courage & Calling

» Biography.com Editors & Tyler Piccotti. **"Harriet Tubman."** *Biography.com*, updated December 11, 2023. https://www.biography.com/activists/harriet-tubman?utm_source=chatgpt.com

» National Park Service. **"Harriet Tubman and the Underground Railroad."** U.S. National Park Service. https://www.nps.gov/hatu/index.htm

» National Park Service. **"Harriet Tubman."** People profile, U.S. National Park Service. National Park Service

» *Harriet Tubman quotes* (including "There was such a glory over everything…"). Curated on multiple reputable quote archives. https://www.brainyquote.com/quotes/harriet_tubman_310311?utm_source=chatgpt.com

Strong Black Woman, Mental Health & Rest

» White, Cynthia Nicole. ***When Being Strong Hurts: Trauma and the Strong Black Woman Stereotype.*** Doctoral dissertation, University of South Carolina, 2021. https://scholarcommons.sc.edu/etd/6538/?utm_source=chatgpt.com

» Iheduru-Anderson, K. **"Redefining Strength: Challenging the Strong Black Woman Stereotype and Its Impact on Mental Health."** *Journal of the National Medical Association*, 2025. https://pmc.ncbi.nlm.nih.gov/articles/PMC12489196/?utm_source=chatgpt.com

» Holmes, Chimère G. **"Why the 'Strong Black Woman' Stereotype Is Bad for Black Mental Health."** *Therapy for Black Girls*, March 20, 2021. https://therapyforblackgirls.com/2021/03/20/why-the-strong-black-woman-stereotype-is-bad-for-black-mental-health/?utm_source=chatgpt.com

» The JED Foundation. **"How to Break Free of the 'Strong Black Woman' Stereotype."** JED Foundation mental health resource. https://jedfoundation.org/resource/how-to-break-free-of-the-strong-black-woman-stereotype/?utm_source=chatgpt.com

» **Therapy for Black Girls** – Dr. Joy Harden Bradford's platform and podcast on mental wellness for Black women and girls. https://therapyforblackgirls.com/?utm_source=chatgpt.com

Indigenous Women, Colonialism & Caregiving

» Stinson, Jane. *Local Women Matter #4: How Colonialism Affects Women.* Canadian Research Institute for the Advancement of Women (CRIAW-ICREF), 2016. https://www.criaw-icref.ca/wp-content/uploads/2021/04/Local-Women-Matter-4-How-Colonialism-Affects-Women.pdf?utm_source=chatgpt.com

» McKinley, Crystal et al. **"All Work and No Play: Indigenous Women 'Pulling the Weight' in Home Life."** *Sex Roles*, 2021. https://pmc.ncbi.nlm.nih.gov/articles/PMC8321394/?utm_source=chatgpt.com

» Glover, R. **"Indigenous Motherwork in Crisis: Caregiving, Resistance and Community Survival During the COVID-19 Pandemic."** *Sex Roles*, 2025. https://link.springer.com/article/10.1007/s11199-025-01584-4?utm_source=chatgpt.com

» Palmar Uriana, D. **"Discrimination Against Wayuu Women as a System of Oppression."** *The Journal of International Perspectives on Justice*, 2024. https://digital.sandiego.edu/cgi/viewcontent.cgi?article=1103&context=ipj-research&utm_source=chatgpt.com

Latinas, Marianismo & Caregiving

» Mendez-Luck, Carolyn A., & Katherine P. Anthony. **"Marianismo and Caregiving Role Beliefs Among U.S.-Born and Immigrant Mexican Women."** *The Journals of Gerontology: Series B*, 71(5), 926–935, 2016. https://pubmed.ncbi.nlm.nih.gov/26362602/

» Mendez-Luck, Carolyn A., et al. **"Orientation to the Caregiver Role Among Latinas of Mexican Origin."** *The Gerontologist*, 56(6), e99–e108, 2016. https://pubmed.ncbi.nlm.nih.gov/27342443/

» Blossom, Priscilla. **"We Need To Talk About Marianismo."** *HipLatina*, March 13, 2018. https://hiplatina.com/marianismo/?utm_source=chatgpt.com

South Asian & Asian Immigrant Women

» Division on South Asian Americans (DoSAA), Asian American Psychological Association. ***Immigrant South Asian Women in the United States: Fact Sheet for Mental Health Practitioners.*** 2018. https://aapaonline.org/wp-content/uploads/2018/05/DoSAA-SAsian-Immigrant-Women-Factsheet-2018.pdf?utm_source=chatgpt.com

» Grahame, Kamini Maraj. **"'For the Family:' Asian Immigrant Women's Triple Day."** *Journal of Sociology & Social Welfare*, 30(1), 65–90, 2003.